The Future of the Oceans

A Report to the Club of Rome

Elisabeth Mann Borgese

Harvest House
WITHDRAWN
MONTREAL

Deposited in the Bibliothèque Nationale of Quebec, 3rd Quarter 1986.

Typography and Cover: Naoto Kondo

Printed in Canada

First Harvest House Edition

For information address:
Harvest House Ltd., 1200 Atwater Ave, Suite #1
Montréal, Canada H3Z 1X4

Canadian Cataloguing in Publication Data

Borgese, Elisabeth Mann
The future of the oceans: a report to the Club of Rome

Includes index.
Bibliography: p.
ISBN 0-88772-220-2

1. Marine resources conservation—Law and legislation.
2. Marine resources. I. Club of Rome II. Title.

JX4411.B67 1986   341.7'62   C86-090193-9

Our whole attitude toward the oceans
must change.

Luis Echeverria
PRESIDENT OF MEXICO

Contents

	Foreword	ix
	Abbreviations	xvi
	Introduction	1
ONE:	Ocean Sciences: New Perspectives	5
TWO:	The Marine Revolution	13
THREE:	The Economics of The Common Heritage	43
FOUR:	A Constitution for the Oceans: Systems-Maintaining	69
FIVE:	A Constitution for the Oceans: Systems-Transforming	93
SIX:	The Philosophy of the Common Heritage	125
	Notes	135
	Select Bibliography	137
	Index	139

Foreword

Despite the global nature of its concerns, the Club of Rome has hitherto issued reports relevant to the conditions that prevail on only 28 percent of the earth's surface area—dry land—and has neglected consideration of the far larger, water-covered regions. This volume is a first attempt to reestablish a balance. Aurelio Peccei, late president of the Club of Rome, commissioned this study on the future of the oceans by Professor Elisabeth Mann Borgese. And, although he did not live to read the product, I am sure that he would have found it enthralling and stimulating.

From time immemorial humans have sensed wonder and mystery in the seeming endlessness of the oceans and have expressed curiosity in what lay beyond. The oceans have also represented the greatest challenge of nature, leading heroes, from the earliest times, to struggle against the tides and tempests in their voyages of trade, fishing, or exploration. Later it was recognized that life originated in the oceans, and even more recently the discoveries of oceanographers began to reveal the previously concealed morphology of the seabed with its mountains and canyons.

In recent years interest in the seas has accelerated greatly, fostered by three reasons. First, the findings of both physical and biological oceanography have advanced to the point that we now have a coherent, detailed picture of the oceans and their creatures. Indeed, we can now envision the planetary system as a whole, as well as the relations between land, sea, and the atmosphere, and the climatic consequences of their interactions. Undersea exploration has yielded a fascinating and even awesome picture of the geoprocesses in operation over the eons. The continental drift and inexorable moving of the tectonic plates represent geophysical and geochemical forces on a scale far greater than that of our experience on the land surface. Likewise, undersea exploration has exposed completely new biological systems. For example, the recent discovery of oases in the desert of the deep sea—the Pacific trough westward of the Galapagos Islands—totally separated from the rest of organic nature and to which no light penetrates and hence no photosynthesis is possible, is one of the most dramatic findings of recent years. This discovery indicates the presence of thermal seepages from the earth's interior, carrying not only heat but also many chemical elements to the ocean depths, and the emergence of strange species which appear to have adapted to life on a sulphur metabolism.

The second reason for greater interest in the seas arises from a new appreciation of the economic potential of the oceans. Fisheries were, of course, one of the earliest sources of food, but until very recently they remained at the hunting and gathering stage of human activity, which was abandoned millennia ago on land with the rise of settled agriculture. It is true, of course, that the "weapons" of the sea hunters have been greatly improved as technology has advanced. For example, ships have been designed that can fish thousands of miles from their land base, and sonar and radar devices are being used to detect shoals of fish. However, this combination of primitive husbandry and modern technology has led to overfishing, depletion of stocks, and even threat to the survival of some species, including the great whales. Now, with an understanding of the dynamics of fish populations, their relationship with their food supplies, and the need for conservation, fishing is at last passing into the settled stage reached long ago by agriculture.

Until recently the economic potential of the oceans was considered only in terms of their biological riches—fish, whales, seaweeds, etc.—as well as their importance as a means of communication from one land mass to the others. Now this potential has been extended to other dimensions. As the demand for petroleum increased and most of the terrestrial deposits were identified and exploited, exploration for oil was extended to the continental shelf and new technology was developed for its recovery. The discovery of manganese nodules consisting of mixtures of many valuable metals is leading to enormous commercial interest in seabed minerals, which may become valuable as the richer of the terrestrial ores become exhausted and lower-grade ores more costly to beneficiate become the only alternative.

The third contemporary reason for interest in the oceans is, sadly, their military significance. While naval warfare has long played an important role in the historical power struggles, modern military technology has given this kind of warfare a new dimension. Nuclear and other kinds of submarines, sophisticated detection devices, and the possibility of using fast, mobile undersea vessels for launching nuclear missiles have transformed the nature of warfare on and under the sea. Furthermore, especially for the superpowers and a few other of the highly industrialized nations, these developments are making dominance of the oceans an important aspect of power politics.

World "Problematique"

It is both this aspect of the multifarious uses of the oceans and the enormous variety of properties that they offer that make this subject so central to the Club of Rome's concept of the world "problematique." By this we mean the tangle of problems and issues that are interconnected and interacting by some obvious, but many more obscurely sensed, mechanisms. These problems and issues constitute the contemporary difficulties of society, and their interactions make it increasingly impossible to deal with them separately and sequentially.

The oceans involve economic, military, and power problems. Moreover, they constitute an exceedingly important proportion of the physical and biological resources available to us. Their use as a sink for the waste products of the industrial and consumer societies and the attendant pollution problems pose an eventual threat to the health of the planet. And, finally, their importance in determining the climate and its regularities across the planet is great although dimly understood.

These and many other aspects of the marine environment demand much more study and research and substantial agreement and action on an international level. As one example of the uncertainties involved, there is at present much public concern over the increased carbon dioxide content of the atmosphere, caused by burning of fossil fuels and decreased adsorption by green plants as a result of the cutting down of large areas of tropical forests. Many outstanding meteorologists feel that these developments will lead in a few decades' time, through the so-called "greenhouse effect," to a virtually irreversible heating of the surface of the planet. This will, in turn, lead to radical changes in the thermal currents and rainfall distribution and to general climatic change as well. This effect may also lead to a significant rise in sea level if the heating, which will be greater at the poles than at the equator, results in the melting of vast masses of ice.

The main zone of ignorance in this complex matter relates to the extent to which the oceans will absorb the carbon dioxide, transforming it chemically into carbonates on the ocean floor. Clearly, this serious problem, with grave consequences for agriculture and life styles, raises basic questions concerning the energy policies of the future. It is also one that cannot be solved by the action of individual countries in isolation.

Law of the Sea

Increasing recognition of the potential of the ocean naturally raises serious questions about the distribution of power, control over the seas, and the right to exploit its resources.

Foreword

This could well lead to eternal struggles between nations over terrestrial rights being extended to 72 percent of the marine surface and to the riches of the ocean and the seabed. These riches, then, would be exploited essentially by the industrialized countries possessing the technology and capital to do so, to the detriment of the poor, less-developed nations of the world. Until recently the oceans were regarded as the global commons, with countries claiming sovereignty only over waters within three miles of their shores. In recent years, however, there has been a tendency for countries to claim jurisdiction over sea areas much farther from land, to protect rich fisheries, and to stake claims to potential offshore oil reserves on the continental shelf. This then led to a series of Law of the Sea conferences—a seemingly endless discussion, often marked by chauvinistic bickering and short-term national selfishness—which finally resulted in adoption of a comprehensive convention. Professor Borgese played an exceedingly important role in the initiation of these talks, working closely with Arvid Pardo who, as Ambassador of Malta to the United Nations, was able to bring world attention to the need for renegotiation of the marine rights of nations.

There is much public ignorance about the outcome of the United Nations Conference on the Law of the Sea and about the significance of the Convention. This book, as far as I am aware, is the first attempt to give both a clear indication of what was, in fact, agreed and, more important, its real significance. Specifically, Chapters 1 and 2 describe the value and potentials of the oceans, while Chapters 3–6 cover the legal, social, economic, and ideological problems posed, the agreements achieved, and what they should mean in practice.

On the whole, Professor Borgese is more optimistic about the outcome of the Conference than I would have suspected. She puts great store in the significance of the international area, beyond the extended territorial and economic limits, and of the international arrangements for their management and exploitation. This is the first example, on a large scale, of full international management of an area of the world's surface based on a system of nonownership, and it is exceedingly important that it succeed. Not only would its success be in the interest of the landlocked and the less-developed nations, it could also serve as a precedent for other international negotiations which may be looming, such as those on the future status of Antarctica.

Elisabeth Mann Borgese's achievements with regard to the marine environment are by no means restricted to the influence she has had on the development of the Law of the Sea. In a very successful series of the now fourteen Pacem in Maribus conferences which she has organized, every aspect of the oceans has been discussed, and these meetings have done much to heighten interest in marine problems and possibilities. She is currently chairman of the Planning Council of the International Ocean Institute, Malta.

Professor Borgese's concern for the oceans is as vast and as deep as the oceans themselves, and her knowledge and understanding of the problems and interaction of problems are outstanding. Thus the Club of Rome greatly welcomes this volume, the eleventh report submitted to it, and recommends it for widespread attention.

Alexander King
President, Club of Rome

Acknowledgments

The author is grateful to UNESCO for the permission to include chapter Six in this volume, the ideas for which were first developed in a study commissioned by UNESCO in the context of its project on the Rights of Future Generations.

Thanks are also due to Arvid Pardo, Jan Tinbergen, Jovan Djordjević and Orio Giarini, whose works have inspired this writing.

This book has been published with the help of a grant from the Social Science Federation of Canada, using funds provided by the Social Sciences and Humanities Research Council of Canada.

Abbreviations

COFI	Committee on Fisheries (FAO)
D&P	dowry and patrimony
ECLA	Economic Commission for Latin America
EEC	European Economic Community
EEZ	Exclusive Economic Zone
FAO	Food and Agriculture Organization of the United Nations
GNP	gross national product
IAEA	International Atomic Energy Agency
ILO	International Labour Organisation
IMO	International Maritime Organization
IOC	Intergovernmental Oceanographic Commission
ISA	International Sea-Bed Authority
JEFERAD	Joint Venture for Exploration, Research and Development
NASA	National Aeronautics and Space Administration
NOAA	National Oceanic and Atmospheric Administration
OETB	Ocean Economics and Technology Branch
OTEC	Ocean Thermal Energy Conversion
UNCLOS	United Nations Conference on the Law of the Sea
UNCTAD	United Nations Conference on Trade and Development
UNDP	United Nations Development Programme
UNEP	United Nations Environment Programme
UNESCO	United Nations Educational, Scientific and Cultural Organization
UNIDO	United Nations Industrial Development Organization
WHO	World Health Organization
WMO	World Meteorological Organization

Introduction

Almost two decades have passed since the Government of Malta took the historic initiative in the United Nations of proposing a new order for the oceans. This order is based on the principle that the deep seabed, beyond the limits of national jurisdiction, is the common heritage of mankind, to be used and exploited only for peaceful purposes and for the benefit of all mankind.

Perhaps even more amazing than Malta's initiative was the fact that the international community represented at the United Nations followed the lead of Malta, its second smallest and most recent member, and elaborated and adopted a United Nations Convention on the Law of the Sea. The Convention declares the seabed and its resources beyond the limits of national jurisdiction to be the common heritage of mankind, establishes the International Sea-Bed Authority to manage this common heritage for the benefit of all, provides a general framework for other uses of the seas, introduces a comprehensive international environmental law, and creates a binding dispute settlement system.

Together with the Convention, the United Nations Conference on the Law of the Sea also adopted a number of resolutions. Two of these are of particular practical importance. Resolution II establishes an interim regime for deep-sea exploration, research, and development for "pioneer investors," that is, states and companies that have already invested large amounts of money in ocean mining and need certain guarantees in the interim period between the adoption of the Convention and its coming into force. Resolution I establishes a Preparatory Commission to administer this regime and to prepare for early operation

1

of the new institutions (International Sea-Bed Authority and International Tribunal for the Law of the Sea) established by the Convention.

All this occurred at a time when most other efforts to create a new international economic order had failed, the gap between poor and rich countries had widened, the global economic and financial system was teetering on the brink of disaster, starvation was rampant, the arms race had escalated, and the fuse of war was lit in Lebanon and Nicaragua, in Afghanistan and Poland, and in Argentina and Grenada—in so many places that the final explosion seemed inevitable.

Thus on the micro scale of a twenty-year period was evident what has been evident on the macro scale of history all along. That is, in spite of accumulated scientific insights, technical skills, and control over the environment, mankind is not getting any better or happier, nor, perhaps, any worse or unhappier.

Thus this book is not inspired by cornucopian visions, nor does it place blind faith in the "technology fix." For every problem solved, two new ones will undoubtedly arise, like Hydra heads. Yet some problems can be solved.

The oceans have been chosen as a great laboratory for making a new order for a variety of reasons which, taken together, create a unique situation. Dramatic advances in the marine sciences are changing our concept of the planet Earth and man's place on it. Marine technology is available to generate and utilize new living, nonliving, and energy resources which could make a significant contribution toward solving the world's food and energy problems, among others.

Marine resource management and the conservation of the marine environment are inextricably intertwined. The integration of economics and ecology could give rise to a new economic theory—the economics of the common heritage— which is urgently needed as neither capitalism nor communism appears capable of coping with the global economic crisis.

The new Law of the Sea, which embodies—no matter how timidly or inadequately during its first phase—the principle of the common heritage of mankind, has triggered trends in the direction of new institutional forms of international cooperation in the marine sector, with inevitable consequences for the rest of the international system.

Marine sciences and technology, marine economy, the Law of the Sea, and its embodiment in a new institutional framework all emanate from, postulate, and contribute to a new ideology—a new ecological world view—apt to enhance development, equity, and peace.

The new Law of the Sea is based on the awareness that the problems of the oceans are closely interrelated and must be considered as a whole, not more, but not less, than a special application of an insight first gained by Buddha 2,500 years ago and most recently articulated by systems theory: "As a net is made up by a series of knots," Buddha taught, "so everything in this world is connected by a series of knots. If anyone thinks that the mesh of a net is an independent, isolated thing, he is mistaken."

Understanding the linkages, causalities, effects, and feedbacks between all these meshes is beyond the capacity of the most powerful computer programmed by the most brilliant systems analyst. Thus we do not know what effects problems solved in the ocean laboratory will have on the rest of the global system or "net." Solutions to problems in the oceans may be—and, indeed, have been—frustrated by the negative impact made by a series of unfortunate developments and trends in the rest of the world. However, if we continue to be more or less successful in dealing with the oceans, there may be a breakthrough, and the new order in the oceans might have a significant impact on the rest of the system. We may even solve some of the most terrible problems, such as hunger or the arms race, development, and disarmament. We must not have the illusion, however, that by solving some problems we shall not create others.

This book attempts a very succinct, synoptic analysis of the scientific, technical, economic, legal, institutional, and ideological aspects of the ongoing "marine revolution." The adoption in 1982 of the United Nations Convention on the Law of the Sea—which had been signed by 159 states by the end of 1984—and the establishment of a new ocean regime create a most suitable platform from which to attempt this overview. New options, new challenges, new dangers, all of which have the same bewildering dimensions as the opportunities, appear on the horizon.

ONE

Ocean Sciences:

New Perspectives

Human thought was mythical and poetic before it turned scientific. But scientific thought has retained and revalidated much of the ancient mythological and poetic concept. A part of science itself, in every age, is shown by subsequent ages to have been poetry or myth.

The maps designed by ancient civilizations were pieces of art, myth, and intuition. Through the millennia, however, they gradually reflected and projected more scientific insight into the planetary system; mathematics; exploration, discovery, and conquest; and the growing intricacies and complexities of human life—of cities, boundaries, traffic nets, population densities, resources, climates, economic activities.

The maps of the oceans were flat and blue, dotted here and there by an island, real or imaginary. The floor was known to be deep below. It was thought to be flat, a vast plain, inhabited by monsters, if at all.

Throughout antiquity people believed that one ocean ringed the earth as it was then known. It was not until the dawn of the modern age that the contours of the seas began to take their present form. Amazingly, it was only during the twentieth century that the ocean floor began to yield its secrets. Mountains, canyons, deep trenches, and fire-spewing volcanoes emerged from the darkness.

Marine sciences and technology—sonar, laser technology, holography, magnetology, seismology, deep-sea photography, and television—received a big boost from military research in World War II. Just after the war a series of magnificent maps of the ocean floor began to be published, largely in the United States and the Soviet Union, the superpowers in deep-ocean research. Like the backbone of a giant reptile, the mid-ocean ridge curved beneath the world ocean. Forty thousand miles long, this mountain chain was far longer, and had peaks far taller, than anything on earth. Transverse faults attached to the giant backbone like rib cages. A new world was discovered on which our known world of continents floated like a minor and fleeting incident.

Although they were works of art, scientific creativeness, and imagination, the maps were still in a primitive stage, considering that only 3 percent of the ocean floor had really been explored. The marine cartographers of the 1980s look at those of the 1960s and 1970s as the latter may have looked at the cartographers of earlier centuries. The computerization of seismic, acoustic, and magnetic data has once more revolutionized our concept of the ocean floor, revealing distortions and closing gaps. It has also confirmed and refined the theory of plate tectonics and continental drift which, on the basis of Genesis, was first intuited by religious thinkers in the seventeenth century, was proposed as a semiscientific theory by the German meteorologist and explorer Alfred Wegener in 1912, and elaborated, with the help of the new scientific-technological arsenal, by U.S., Canadian, and British scientists in the 1950s and 1960s.

Thus as we now know, the mid-ocean ridges are cleft lengthwise by a deep rift from which molten basalt pours forth from the earth's mantle, enlarging the crust on a spreading ocean floor. During a human life the floor moves, roughly speaking, the length of a human body. In this way oceans grow and continents are forced apart. The continents, having granitic rock lighter than the basaltic rock of the ocean floor, slide on vast tectonic plates on the basalt ground. They separate, and sometimes they clash. When

6

continents clash, mountains pile up, pushing submarine surfaces high into the sky.

This shifting of land masses is presently causing some bodies of water, such as the Atlantic Ocean and the Red Sea, to expand. Other bodies, such as the Pacific Ocean and the Mediterranean Sea, are slowly disappearing. Oceans expand from the center, their floor spreading from the magma-spewing, mid-ocean rift. They shrink from the margin, where a system of deep trenches devours ocean floor faster than it is produced at the center. The floor sinks into these maws. The earth quakes, and its molten core slaps over the rims of volcanoes all along island arches that accompany the deep trenches.

Every 300–400 million years, the earth is made over, inside out and outside in, like kneaded bread dough. Only the continents, which are too light to be sucked into the trenches, remain floating outside on their tectonic plates, like bits of foam—merging, separating, turning around, and changing climes, flora, and fauna.

In refining and deepening this theory, and bolstering it with masses of new data processed on microchips, two startling new discoveries were made: one geological in nature; the other, biological.

Geological Discovery

In 1981, the U.S. National Oceanic and Atmospheric Administration (NOAA) announced the discovery of massive polymetallic sulphide deposits on the East Pacific Rise, the Galapagos Ridge, and the Juan de Fuca Ridge. These deposits were formed when the cold bottom seawater, which has percolated into the ocean crust through cracks and crevices for millions of years, slowly reacted with the rock in the crust. This happens at the bottom of the sea just as it may happen between rainwater and terrestrial rock. Rainwater sometimes seeps some thirty to fifty kilometers into the ground and returns to the surface as thermal springs. As it is heated by volcanic rock, the seawater absorbs heavy metals. The hot brine, with its heavy metal content, eventually returns to the ocean floor through hydrothermal vents or "smokers." There it mixes with the cold bottom water, and the metals are precipitated and sedimented.

Alexander Malahoff, NOAA's chief scientist, reported that the Galapagos Ridge polymetallic sulphides contain 11 percent copper and up to 0.8 percent zinc, with minor constituents of silver, lead, molybdenum, and tin.

These deposits are structurally identical to the Cyprus copper mines which formed some 50–100 million years ago and provided the basis for the Copper Age of human civilization. Throughout history these mines were considered a "nonrenewable" resource. They were mined out and exhausted in Cyprus as well as at other sites on earth. Indeed, the 1960s and 1970s were characterized by an increasing nervousness and fear that our wasteful industrial society would, in the predictable and rather imminent future, simply run out of nonrenewable resources.

The deposits discovered on the Pacific Ocean floor, though identical in structure to terrestrial deposits, turned out to be a mere one hundred years old, offering an unprecedented opportunity to study metallogenesis on earth. Some of the massive deposits in the deep-sea environment had formed within a decade: a renewable resource! In this sense, Malahoff[1] suggested that " 'harvesting' of ocean floor polymetallic sulphide deposits may become a more appropriate term in the future than 'mining.' "

Now that scientists know where and how to look for them, new discoveries have been made in rapid succession off the coasts of Oregon and Washington and of British Columbia. As Canadian scientist B.D. Lonkarevic[2] has speculated, such deposits "might occur anywhere along the 70,000 km long chain of mid-ocean mountains. If this is the case, the amount of metals available to the miners of the future is truly staggering. Simply beyond comprehension. Even speculation about the exploitation of this resource would sound like science fiction today."

The fact that heavy metals poured into the oceans from the interior of the earth for millions of years was not known in the 1960s and early 1970s, when a number of studies began to be made on the impact of human activities on the ocean environment, such as pollution with heavy metals. Obviously this impact is different if one takes into account the natural inputs, and it may have to be reassessed. This does not mean, of course, that the impact of human activities should be neglected and that environmental concerns should be put aside, as suggested by some reactions to the current economic recession and the recent backlash to the environmental movement of the 1970s. Locally, man-made pollution may be far more important than natural pollution, as it includes materials that do not exist in nature. Thus introduction of these materials into the marine environment may have consequences that we are unable to assess.

Clearly, oceanography has done more than deepen our understanding of the oceans, it has also changed our perception of the planet and of its continuous evolution and transformation. Moreover, it has changed our notion of "resources." Resources—even nonrenewable resources—can no longer be considered as something given, static, once and for all. In the final analysis, there is no such thing as a "nonrenewable" resource. Resources recycle as the earth remakes itself. For human use, resources are increasingly what science and technology make them to be.

Territorial conquest and expansion of national jurisdiction appear to be based on the obsolete, static concept of a resource as something given and possessed. Scientific and technological cooperation in understanding the genesis of resources and how to create them does not call for national aggrandizement and seems much more in line with the new oceanography.

Biological Discovery

The second staggering discovery was that there are forms of life at the bottom of the sea which are fundamentally different from life on earth.

The above-mentioned smokers or hydrothermal vents, spewing hot water like geysers, are like heat oases in a desert of cold. And they are teeming with life—flourishing crab populations and large white clams, some almost a foot long. The surface of the lava pillows characterizing these sites have been found encrusted with white-tubed serpulid polychaetes. There are also small, light-colored, eel-like fish and various kind of limpets, as well as giant tube worms which cluster around the warm water vents. Two to three centimeters in diameter, these worms can reach a length of up to three meters, making them the largest worms ever found. They wear red, gill-like crowns.

The strangest thing about these animals is that their growth, and their existence, is not based on photosynthesis but on the quite different, almost unearthly, principle of chemosynthesis. This process is effected by bacteria which constitute the basic foodstuff of this ecological system or, more correctly, the basis of a symbiotic relationship. These animals largely consist of bacteria. As UNESCO's *Ocean Science for the Year 2000*[3] points out, "the structuring of these communities on a primary production source provided by chemo-autotrophic bacteria has been suggested to be analogous to the communities which may have existed in the geological past before the evolution of photosynthesis."

Thus in the depths of the oceans where primordial transformations keep recycling and renewing the substance of our planet, we may have found the origin of life, showing again that, from a scientific point of view, the oceans are our great laboratory. "Biological oceanography provides a rich source of ideas and concepts for general biology that may prove to have much wider application," *Ocean Science for the Year 2000*[3] points out. "Marine ecosystems are less perturbed and easier to understand than terrestrial ecosystems. . . . The exploration of new conceptual models of marine ecosystems will inevitably have important influences on the development of terrestrial ecology."

Understanding Marine Ecology

Understanding of marine ecology requires international, multidisciplinary, cooperative research. In this respect, the marine sciences are at the forefront, moving in a direction in which more and more science will have to go. For not only must we study the interactions of species, we must also study the interactions between the living systems with their environment and the ocean's chemistry—its physical parameters, waves, currents, and tides—and the interactions between the water and the atmosphere.

The links between marine bioecosystems and the ocean-atmosphere interaction recently received special emphasis in connection with the phenomenon known as El Niño. Traditionally thought to be simply a local phenomenon off the Peruvian and Ecuadorian coasts that temporarily halted the upwelling of cold, nutritious bottom waters on which fish and bird life depends, El Niño is now recognized as having worldwide ramifications. This then is just one more illustration of the need for a global, comprehensive view of the world ocean, where problems are closely interrelated and must be considered as a whole.

Investigations of the phenomenon of El Niño have revealed that the well-being of Peruvian fishermen is in fact linked to autumnal low-pressure regions in Indonesia and Australia, which generate the trade winds. These winds drive surface water from the equatorial Pacific in the direction of Australia, raising the water level in these regions. To compensate, cold bottom water flows in the opposite direction and is forced up along the eastern rim of the Pacific. Thus one can envisage these winds driving and turning the South Pacific like an enormous wheel.

When the low-pressure zones in Australia and Indonesia fail to materialize, the wheel stops and surface waters begin to warm. Sometimes the wind even blows in the opposite direction, piling warm surface waters near the Peruvian coast.

One can imagine the global impact of changes of this magnitude. Their links to monsoons in Southeast Asia, droughts in Australia and in the Sahel, grain production in North America, and storms in Europe have been demonstrated over the past two years, as El Niño of 1982–1983 was the largest recorded in 150 years.

Thus, as illustrated above, the marine sciences, by their very nature, are as globe-spanning as the oceans. They drive the scientist, as irresistibly as the wind, in the direction of global, interdisciplinary cooperation and force on us new concepts about the earth, its genesis and evolution, and the origin of life.

TWO

The Marine Revolution

A number of excellent books have been written over the past ten years on the diversification and intensification of uses of the ocean, and all authors agree that the oceans are playing an increasingly important role in world economics and in the economies of states (see Select Bibliography).

Changes in the uses of the oceans, in technological, economic, and political terms, have been all-pervasive and systems-transforming.

The users of the oceans are no longer just a handful of maritime powers but the world community as a whole. Every country, whether developed or developing, coastal or landlocked, has a stake in the oceans today.

The security of the oceans may be threatened by the new, critical role they are playing in global strategy. For example, they can serve as a hiding place for submarines armed with intercontinental ballistic missiles which can reach any spot on earth. Thus the oceans have become the hub of the balance of terror and a repository for the superpowers' second-strike (and first-strike) capabilities.

Every country, whether coastal or landlocked, also depends on the ocean for its trade, now carried by multimodal systems of transport comprising sea routes as well as land routes and linked by the new technology of container shipping. Any landlocked commercial center can now become a container terminal or nodal point in world shipping. This transformation of the world's shipping industry, symbolizing the integration of marine and terrestrial production systems, may have as yet unknown consequences.

This chapter highlights three developments of the marine revolution—that is, the penetration of the industrial revolution into the oceans. These developments appear to have the greatest long-term potential and are likely to contribute most to the ongoing transformation of human society.

Aquaculture

From an anthropological perspective, the advent of aquaculture may turn out to be as important as the advent of agriculture ten thousand years ago.

Aquaculture—the cultivating of aquatic plants and the husbanding of aquatic animals—has roots deep in the past. The Chinese and Indians practiced it thousands of years ago, and their expertise in hydroengineering, including pond construction, as well as their knowledge of fish and how to feed and care for them, were truly astounding. Despite these accomplishments, however, aquaculture remained static like the societies that gave birth to it, and it failed to expand beyond those historic limits.

It was only in the 1960s that aquaculture began to assume worldwide dimensions, and it was not until the 1980s that its enormous importance and potential were generally recognized (Table 1). During these two decades, the contribution of aquaculture to total fisheries production rose from negligible to 15 percent, and it continues to increase by about 10 percent annually, whereas fishing from the wild is stagnant or recessive.

Species after species of aquatic plant or animal has offered the same scenario. Catches, or harvest, from the wild have declined due to overexploitation, pollution, or causes beyond human control (hydrological or climatological changes), and culture is undertaken on an experimental basis. At the beginning, production from culture is marginal. Over a period of fifteen to twenty years, however,

14

TABLE 1

Aquaculture production by region and commodity groups, 1980 (metric tons)

Country	Total	Finfish	Mollusks	Crustaceans	Seaweeds
Africa					
Cent. African Rep.	67	67			
Egypt	2,597	2,597			
Gabon	10	10			
Ghana	120	120			
Ivory Coast	50	50			
Lesotho	27	27			
Malawi	92	92			
Morocco	140		140		
Rwanda	19	19			
South Africa	646	315	331		
Tunisia	60	60			
Zaire	704	704			
Total	4,532	4,061	471		
Asia and Oceania					
Australia	8,150		8,150		
Bangladesh	65,000	65,000			
China	4,012,102	813,320	1,757,960		1,440,822
Cyprus	30	30			
Hong Kong	7,490	7,260	230		
India	848,973	830,201	1,763	17,009	
Indonesia	199,297	177,500		21,797	
Israel	14,580	14,580			
Japan	976,140	249,397	298,231	2,468	426,044
Korea, Rep.	481,480	943	284,749	125	195,663
Malaysia	73,741	9,357	63,412	972	
Nepal	5,200	5,200			
New Zealand	5,002	2	5,000		
Papua New Guinea	60	60			
Philippines	285,502	151,612	250	910	132,730
Singapore	536	497		39	
Sri Lanka	17,150	17,150			
Syria	1,180	1,180			
Taiwan	183,673	127,974	37,507	7,017	11,175
Thailand	160,962	39,367	111,673	9,923	
Turkey	5,573	5,573			
Total	7,351,821	2,516,203	2,568,925	60,260	2,206,434
Europe					
Austria	3,200	3,200			
Bulgaria	22,874	22,824			50
Czechoslovakia	14,193	14,193			

TABLE 1 *(Continued)*

Country	Total	Finfish	Mollusks	Crustaceans	Seaweeds
Denmark	17,111	17,111			
Finland	3,195	3,195			
France	198,375	25,345	173,000	30	
German Dem. Rep.	12,634	12,634			
Germany, Fed. Rep.	24,880	13,120	11,760		
Greece	1,800	1,800			
Hungary	26,470	26,470			
Ireland	570	570			
Italy	78,000	28,236	49,764		
Netherlands	98,489		98,489		
Norway	7,513	7,513			
Poland	12,100	12,100			
Romania	41,325	41,325			
Spain	194,460	24,460	170,000		
Sweden	2,000	500	1,500		
Switzerland	1,500	1,500			
U.K.	5,813	5,000	813		
USSR	340,000	340,000			
Yugoslavia	29,290	29,100	190		
Total	1,135,792	630,196	505,516	30	50
Latin America and Caribbean					
Argentina	2,000	2,000			
Bolivia	50	50			
Chile	1,478	328	1,150		
Colombia	400	400			
Costa Rica	100	100			
Cuba	6,500	3,800	2,700		
Dominican Rep.	906	906			
Ecuador	4,600			4,600	
El Salvador	39	39			
Jamaica	44	44			
Mexico	55,752	17,198	38,554		
Panama	375	15		360	
Peru	850	450		400	
Venezuela	2,150	150	2,000		
Total	75,244	25,480	44,404	5,360	
North America					
Canada	4,567	1,739	2,828		
United States	135,407	55,646	74,165	5,596	
Total	139,974	57,386	76,993	5,596	
Grand total	8,707,363	3,233,326	3,196,308	71,245	2,206,484

Source: T. V. R. Pillay. Opening Address, *Proceedings of the World Aquaculture Conference, Venice, 1981.* (In press)

the culture is commercialized and production expands, while production from the wild becomes marginal. At the end of the period, the species has been domesticated.

Fifteen to twenty years are required for any innovation to assert itself over and against what systems analysts call the market inertia, investment inertia, and management inertia. Once an innovation, in the form of a new technology, has captured about 5 percent of the market, it is likely to take over altogether—unless another technology is introduced that crowds the first one out.

Aquaculture has now taken over 15 percent of the market, and thus it is safe to predict that it will supersede the hunting and gathering stage, just as agriculture did on land. This is not to say that the oceans will be divided into neat little fenced seafarms. Rather, there will be human intervention at least once, and probably more often, in the life cycle of all commercially harvested species.

Nor is it to say that this development should signify the end of catching fish in the open ocean. Capture will increasingly be part of a more complex process and it will always be preceded by culture. Capture will be just a phase of aquaculture.

The reasons for the advent of aquaculture are numerous and complex.

The increased food requirement of a growing world population is certainly one reason. It is true that the recurring food crises and chronic undernourishment found in so many parts of the world are not due so much to a lack of food resources as to deficiencies in their distribution. However, since food shortages occur in poor countries which depend to a far greater degree on fish for their protein supply than do the carnivorous rich countries, it is obvious that a substantial increase in fish production through aquaculture could make a crucial contribution to solving the problem of hunger.

Lack of agricultural space is another reason for the expansion of aquaculture. Sprawling urbanization, soil erosion, and desertification combine to reduce arable land by millions of hectares per year, and at a time when an increase in food production of at least 3.5 percent per year would be needed just to keep up with the increase in the world population. The more people there are, the more food is needed and the less land is available for food production.

In contrast, the possibilities for expanding aquaculture are, for all practical purposes, unlimited. Aquaculture can be developed in lakes and rivers, reservoirs and irrigation canals, ponds and tanks, rice paddies, estuaries, mangrove swamps, bays, coves and lagoons, inland seas, semi-enclosed seas, and the open ocean. Wherever there is water there should be fish, a Chinese proverb says.

Asia, which accounts for 85 percent of the world's aquaculture production, presently utilizes just two million hectares for this purpose. According to estimates of the U.N. Food and Agriculture Organization (FAO), an additional twenty million hectares are available for development in that area alone. If geographic expansion and even moderate technological improvements are combined, a tenfold increase in aquaculture production by the end of the century may be possible.

Water use can be more intensive than land use for the simple reason that the water body is three-dimensional, permitting polycultures of different, complementary species—carnivores, herbivores, and scavengers; bottom, mid-water, or surface dwellers; fish feeding on the waste products of other fish—and multiple crops. Agricultural space, in contrast, is two-dimensional, usually allowing cultivation of just one crop at a time.

Aquaculture also has a number of other advantages. For example, fish proteins are easier to assimilate than other animal proteins. Furthermore, the cost of producing animal protein from fish is considerably lower than that for producing protein from land animals. More specifically, it costs half as much to produce a ton of protein from fish as from beef and a third as much as from pork. In labor expended, fish requires only a third of the man-hours needed to process pork.

Some forms of aquaculture are extremely capital- and energy-intensive. For example, eel and prawn farming in Japan takes place in totally controlled environments with the water artificially heated and aereated and the feedstuff prepared in computerized factories. In most cases, however, aquaculture is not energy-intensive, giving it an obvious advantage over hunting fish in the wild which, with rising fuel costs, is becoming largely uneconomical.

Although aquaculture will obviously never replace agriculture, they can be beautifully integrated, thereby increasing the productivity of agriculture and adding the crops of aquaculture.

Rice and shrimp production, for example, can be combined in paddie culture and duck and fish production in pond culture. Agricultural wastes can be utilized for pond fertilization, and aquacultural wastes can be used for poultry feed.

Almost any species of aquatic plant or animal can be cultivated, but obviously species that grow quickly, are resistant to diseases, adapt to new environments, and reproduce in captivity are preferred. Once they have been fully domesticated, their useful qualities can be further enhanced through selective breeding or other forms of genetic engineering, which are beginning to be applied to aquaculture. These technologies may increase the growth of aquaculture considerably, as well as the importance of its contribution to the global gross national product (GNP).

Only four species of aquatic plants have been fully domesticated: the red algae *Porphyra* and *Eucheuma* and the brown algae *Laminaria* and *Undaria*. The main producer countries are China *(Laminaria),* Japan *(Porphyra* and *Undaria),* and the Philippines *(Eucheuma).*

Full domestication of aquatic plants passes through three stages: (1) prudent management of natural stocks (e.g., regulating the harvest seasons and harvest techniques); (2) manipulation of the environment (e.g., improving substratum and fertilization and regulating temperature and light); and (3) control of the reproductive process, artificial propagation of seeds and spores, and selective breeding of the plant.

Approximately two million wet tons of seaweed are harvested annually from cultivated and wild sources. The potential for further production is without limit.

Seaweeds are utilized for a variety of purposes. In the Far East, they are raised mostly for food and in the West, for industrial and pharmaceutical purposes. Agar, algin, and carrageenin, which are extracted from seaweed, are used as gels and stabilizers in a variety of industrially prepared foods and medicines and cosmetics as well as in the rubber, textile, paper, and ceramics industries.

Aquatic plants will undoubtedly play an increasingly important role in the production of food, industrial, and pharmaceutical products. In food production we may see a new emphasis on the lower and the lowest trophic levels. For example, tiny one-cell algae such as spirulina grow and multiply at an incredible rate and may be utilized for emergency food production, especially in conjunction with yeast production, and as protein-rich food additives. Only one day is required for the growth of such tiny algae (e.g., chlorella). At the end of the day, one alga divides into two, resulting in four at the end of the second day, eight on the third day, etc. (In a calculable number of days such a tiny alga could, theoretically, produce a mass equal in weight to that of the earth!)

Two other new uses of aquatic plants may be added in the future.

The first is the extraction of energy from aquatic biomass, either in the form of hydrogen, which is a waste product of the metabolism of a strain of blue-green algae, or in the form of methane, which can be extracted from kelp by anaerobic fermentation.

A Japanese researcher at the University of Miami has developed a blueprint for small, individual algae farms—a handy little tank not larger than an oil burner—which could produce all the energy (hydrogen) for an average Florida home. Kelp energy farms, requiring relatively large surfaces of water and capital investment, have been designed and built on a pilot scale in California. Howard A. Wilcox of San Diego, designer of these farms, calculates that they could generate enough energy to fill the requirements of a town of fifty thousand inhabitants. Thus the extraction of energy from aquatic biomass may well be one of the components of a diversified, decentralized, and ecologically balanced energy system of the future.

The second future use of aquatic plants may be in biological systems that extract heavy metal pollutants from water bodies and, conceivably, recycle the metals. The recent discovery by the U.S. National Aeronautics and Space Administration (NASA) that the water hyacinth has the extraordinary capacity to absorb mercury, cadmium, nickel, lead, gold, and silver from industrially polluted water may be a breakthrough in this direction. Plants (as well as bacteria) concentrating such metals may then be accumulated to levels high enough to make pyrometallurgical extraction of the metals economical. The additional discovery that algin has the capacity to concentrate—even extract from the human body—dreaded strontium 90 points in the same direction.

Biological control of pollution fits into a general trend of our time of moving away from mechanical or chemical systems in the direction of biological systems. The potential of bioindustries is indeed enormous, and aquatic plants may play an important role in this context. According to some experts, including Carl Gören Heden of Sweden, this opens new opportunities, particularly for developing countries which could skip directly to the most advanced phase of industrial development.

Another interesting aspect of this development is the merger between farming and mining that it entails. Cultivation of algae, which can be bred selectively to extract and concentrate uranium, is a farming operation. Recovery of the uranium, however, is a mining operation. The uranium farm of the future will be an algae culture, with primary production of uranium and secondary production of methane and fertilizer.

Farming of aquatic animals embraces a wide range and variety of species, from tiny planktonic animals such as brine shrimps, which are raised as a basic feedstuff for a number of "higher" seafarm animals, to larger crustaceans, molluscs, and finfish. One could also well imagine the farming of marine mammals such as dugongs or sea cows.

Like the domestication of aquatic plants, that of animals has gone through various phases. The simplest form of domestication is to trap the young of a species and raise them in a controlled environment until they reach market size. This process is widely practiced with shrimp, milkfish, eel, and even tuna—that is, species that will not breed in captivity. The number of stock available for the harvest depends, however, on chance and on luck in hunting from the wild. This situation changes radically when the final step of domestication is reached, and animals are bred in captivity.

In some species spawning occurs naturally in captivity (e.g., tilapia), while in other species spawning must be induced (e.g., in most carp, shrimp, and milkfish). Spawning can be induced by manipulating the environment (temperature, salinity, current intensity). In shrimp spawning is often induced through eyestalk ablation (the eyestalk, oddly enough, produces a substance that inhibits spawning in captivity), or, most commonly, through the injection of hormones extracted from the pituitary gland (in most carp and, most recently—a breakthrough—in milkfish). The invention of the hormone injection by a Brazilian scientist in the 1930s opened a new chapter in the history of aquaculture. In some highly important commercial species (e.g., eels) induced spawning is not yet possible, and this big industry still depends on the capture of elvers from the wild.

The arsenal of seafarming technology has a number of components. Besides the technology of induced spawning, techniques exist for the care of larvae during the various stages of development and for the preparation of suitable and inexpensive fish feedstuff where this is required. The Chinese, who account for as much as 50 percent of global fish farming production, do not use artificial feedstuffs. They rely entirely on natural farm waste products to feed their fish. Techniques are also available for the construction and maintenance of ponds or other bodies of water suitable for the various stages of the life cycle of aquatic animals (breeding tanks, spawning tanks, hatching containers, nursery ponds, rearing ponds, etc.); for fish veterinary medicine (still in its infancy); for processing and conservation and for the recycling of waste; for the transportation—often across half the globe—of eggs, larvae, or fingerlings; for the transplantation of species, acclimatization, and hybridization; and for polycultures that recreate whole ecosystems of multispecies crops on the basis of recycled waste and the primary production of phytoplankton.

The potential of aquaculture is enormous. If we wanted to gaze into the crystal ball of the future, we might see new developments in the following directions:

— Diversification and intensification of mutually beneficial interactions between aquaculture and agriculture.

— Improvements in induced spawning, applications to new species, and commercialization of seed stock.

— Greater emphasis on the utilization of animals of the lower and lowest trophic levels (krill, even brine shrimp), not only for animal feedstuff but also for direct human consumption, especially as an emergency food supply and as protein-enriching food additives.

— Diversification of cage cultures in lagoons or other protected areas for such species as bream, bass, yellowtail, dorata, trout, tuna, and salmon. Cage culture is the most intensive cost-effective use of water per square meter of surface.

— Diversification and intensification of sea ranching,— that is, the controlled production of fish eggs on land and the rearing of fish larvae and fingerlings until they reach a size at which they can fend successfully against the inclemencies of nature in the open ocean. At this stage they are released into the ocean to reinforce natural stocks. Sea ranching is based on the recognition that, in nature, only one in a thousand fish eggs manages to hatch and reach maturity. Sea ranching may increase this survival ratio a hundredfold.

— Advances in fish behavioral studies and communication with marine animals and control of fish behavior (e.g., devising undersea calls to congregate fish for feeding or stock assessment or to deter fish from determined locations or activities).

The world's fisheries have never contributed more than 3–5 percent to the global GNP. Thus it is no wonder that development economists have tended to downgrade, or outright forget, the oceans when devising development plans. This situation may change radically during the next century with the passage from the hunting and gathering stage to the stage of aquaculture and the development of marine bioindustries. The contribution of the world's fisheries to the GNP might well rise to 15 percent, as a conservative estimate, or to 50 percent or more, as a logical estimate, considering that 80 percent of the globe is covered by water.

Obviously there are constraints on the development of aquaculture as there are on agriculture or on any other human activity, as well as conflicts between uses and between

24

users of aquatic space. New problems will arise as old problems are solved, but aquaculture can contribute to employment in agriculture, in fisheries (where the decline of natural stocks presently creates unemployment), in the processing sector, and in auxiliary industries (freezers, boats, nets, cans, etc.). Production of luxury foods such as cultivated prawns and oysters may earn foreign exchange.

Beyond this, aquaculture represents one of the most significant adaptations of the human race in our age.

Ocean Mining

The second major development of the marine revolution is ocean mining which involves the extraction of minerals and metals from seawater, the seabed, or beneath the ocean floor.

Ocean mining, too, has roots deep in the past. Salt has been extracted from the sea for thousands of years. The kings of India had a "superintendent of ocean mines" as early as the fourth century B.C. This official was responsible for attending to the collection of conch shells, diamonds, precious stones, pearls, corals, and salt and to regulating commerce in these commodities.

Sea coal *(carbo maris)*, mined in England in the thirteenth century, was not only gathered from beaches, it was also excavated from trenches and tunnels. And already Aristotle knew that the ocean water itself contained vast masses of dissolved metal. But to come fully into its own, ocean mining had to await the maturation of oceanography and the development of modern marine technology.

The first major manifestation of the penetration of this branch of the industrial revolution into the oceans was the development of the offshore oil industry.

Offshore oil was first produced in 1894 in California from wells drilled from wooden wharves. However, it was not until the discovery of the Creole field in the Gulf of Mexico in 1934 that offshore oil production began to take off. It took the oil engineering industry nearly twenty years to develop the technology required to drill in 200 meters of water, but when that point was reached, it was as if a barrier had been crashed. Drilling under 400 meters of water was achieved in 1967, and now it can be done at practically any depth.

New drilling structures—jack-up, floating, semisubmersible, and underwater—followed one another in quick succession. The most recent advanced technology is the so-called Underwater Manifold Center Production System recently developed by Shell and Esso for the Cormorant Field in the U.K. sector of the North Sea. This system is installed on the ocean floor, covers an area about half the size of a football field, and is as tall as a four-storey building. It can drill nine wells simultaneously. Most of the components of its control system can be replaced by remote-controlled manipulators (robots). It has been described as a revolution in underwater technique and an extremely important landmark not only in North Sea history but also in world oil production.

The balance of oil power is rapidly shifting, and North Sea reserves now rival those of the Persian Gulf. Exploration extends from the tropical offshore of Africa and South America to the North Atlantic and the Arctic and, soon, to Antarctica.

Even though it is projected to grow at a much slower rate than in the past, world energy demand by the year 2000 is expected to be 65 percent higher than it is today. In spite of conservation, a recession, and the substitution of other energy resources in many sectors of production and communication, oil is expected to remain the major energy source until the end of the century. Total output is estimated to increase from the 1980 level of approximately sixty million barrels per day to about seventy-one million barrels per day about the year 2000 when it will level off (Table 2). Experts estimate that recoverable conventional oil reserves are somewhere on the order of 723 billion barrels, while 550 billion barrels might be avail-

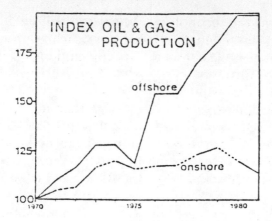

TABLE 2
**World production of crude oil,
total and offshore**

(barrels per day, in thousands)

Year	World production	Offshore production	Offshore as % of world production
1972	49,968.00	8,858.77	17.8
1973	55,212.70	10,067.28	18.2
1974	56,772.00	9,268.62	16.3
1975	53,850.00	8,278.36	15.4
1976	57,210.00	9,431.91	16.5
1977	56,567.00	11,436.75	20.2
1978	60,337.00	11,480.75	19.0
1979	62,768.00	12,491.93	19.9
1980	59,812.00	13,587.49	22.7
1981	55,886.20	13,664.61	24.5
1982	53,191.00	13,521.25	25.4
1983	53,259.00	13,791.04	25.9

Note: 6.998 barrels of crude petroleum equal approximately one metric ton (ASIM-IP petroleum measurement tables).
Source: *Offshore,* June 20, 1977, 1978, 1979, 1980, 1981, 1982, 1983, and July 20, 1984. Tulsa, Oklahoma: Penwell Publishing Co.

able for future discoveries. According to these estimates, there would be enough oil for the next fifty years at present levels of consumption. The total conventional gas reserves (Table 3) are estimated at around 10,500 exajoules (one exajoule is approximately 160 million barrels of oil equivalent).

At least half of these amounts may come from the world's oceans. An estimated fifty thousand square kilometers of land are likely to be oil-bearing and worthy of exploration. Taken together, the planet's offshore regions (shelves,

TABLE 3

**World production of natural gas,
total and offshore**

(cubic feet, in billions)

Year	World production	Offshore production	Offshore as % of world production
1972	43,463.4	6,824.4[a]	15.7
1973	56,992.3	7,697.0	13.5
1974	47,253.3	8,088.7	17.1
1975	47,029.9	9,932.1	20.3
1976	50,407.5	10,847.0[b]	21.5
1977	53,883.7	6,663.3[b]	12.4
1978	53,859.5	9,509.0[b]	17.8
1979	57,194.6	9,369.0[b]	16.4
1980	58,636.4	10,160.9[b]	17.3
1981	57,816.0	10,085.1[b]	17.4
1982	55,893.9	10,357.5[b]	18.5
1983	55,665.0	10,360.1[b]	18.6

[a] Socialist countries not included.
[b] Based on extrapolation from the average daily rate.
Source: Borgese, E.M., and N. Ginsburg, eds. 1985. Ocean Yearbook, Vol. V. Chicago: University of Chicago Press.

slopes, and rises) considered worthy of oil exploration efforts comprise about eighty million square kilometers. Most likely there will be no further growth in land-based oil production. Any increase in production will come from offshore.

Meanwhile, the development of solid mineral and metal mining goes on apace. The exploration and exploitation of offshore sand and gravel, coal, tin, aragonite, gold, platinum, diamonds, ilmenite, rutile, zircon, uranium, and phosphates are expanding farther out and deeper down, as far as the rapidly developing technologies of dredging and tunneling will permit. (Table 4).

The queer-looking dredges built in recent years can literally walk on the seabed, raising one leg and rotating alternately on the other two. Such a dredge walks at a speed of eight meters per hour.

Japan employs eight thousand undersea coal miners who produce about ten million tons of coal from the oceans per year. The mines are too far away from shore to make tunneling from shore practical, so the Japanese built artificial islands from which to drive their shafts into the seabed.

In the 1970s, the German oceanographic ship *Valdivia* explored off the coast of Mozambique and discovered heavy sands at a depth of between twenty and 500 meters. These sands contain about 50 million tons of recoverable ilmenite, 1.5 million tons of rutile, and 4 million tons of zircon, all of which add up to ten times the present annual production of the industrialized world.

These random examples illustrate the abundance of recoverable minerals and metals that enter the oceans from land (erosion, runoffs), from the atmosphere, from outer space, and from the interior of the earth.

The most sophisticated technology has been created for the exploration and exploitation of the polymetallic nodules that litter the seabed of the Pacific, Indian, and Atlantic oceans at a depth of five thousand meters. These nodules contain nickel, copper, cobalt, and manganese, and a

TABLE 4

World annual production of minerals from oceans and beaches
(estimated raw material value in Million U.S. dollars)

	Production value (1972)	Percent value from ocean	Projected production value (1980)
Subsurface soluble minerals and fluids			
Petroleum (oil and gas)	10,300	18	90,000[a]
Frasch sulphur	25	33	
Salt	.1		
Potash (production expected in 1980s)	None		
Geothermal energy	None		
Freshwater springs	35[b]		
Surficial deposits			
Sand and gravel	100	<1	
Lime shells	35	80	
Gold	None		2,000[c]
Platinum	None		
Tin	53	7	
Titanium sands, zircon, and monazite	76	20	
Iron sands	10	<1	
Diamonds (closed down in 1972)	None		
Precious coral	7	100	
Barite	1	3	
Manganese nodules (production expected by early 1980s)			
Phosphorite	None		
Subsurface bedrock deposits			
Coal	335	2	
Iron ore	17	<1	
Extracted from seawater			
Salt	173	29	
Magnesium	75	61	
Magnesium compounds	41	6	
Bromine[d]	<20	30	
Freshwater	51		2,000[c]
Heavy water	27	20	

Others (potassium salts, calcium salts, and sodium sulphate)	1	⎫
Uranium	None	⎬
		⎭
Total		94,000

Note: Total production value of nonpetroleum commodities equals $694 million; total from seawater equals $388 million.

[a] Projections indicate that offshore production by 1980 will probably at least triple the 1972 daily output rate of 9.5 million barrels of oil and 17 billion (10^9) cubic feet of gas per day and that crude oil prices will probably stabilize at around $10 per barrel.

[b] Seawater plant at Freeport, Texas, closed down in late 1969. (U.S. Bureau of Mines. 1973. Mineral Year Book 1971. Washington, D.C.: U.S. Bureau of Mines.)

[c] Also assuming an average 30 percent increase in raw minerals.

[d] More than 200 million gallons of freshwater are recovered per day from submarine springs in Argolis Bay, Greece, but only a small portion of the produced water is utilized.

Source: Govett, G.J.S., and M. H. Govett. 1976. World Mineral Supplies. Amsterdam: Elsevier.

number of other metals. Raising them from that depth is a task comparable to that of having to harvest a field of potatoes on the plain of Lake Geneva from a plane flying high above Mont Blanc at night in a dense fog.

Basically, three different mining systems have been developed. U.S. companies and their partners have developed a vacuum cleaner-type system that lowers a five-kilometer suction pipe from the mining ship to the ocean floor. The Japanese have experimented with a system of continuous line buckets attached to a loop which is kept in place by two mining ships. The buckets sweep over the ocean floor, collect the nodules, bring them up to the ships, empty them, and return to the ocean floor. Finally, the French have developed a system of individual, remote-controlled shuttles which are released from the mining ship, collect the nodules, and return to the ship. Several hundred such shuttles may be involved in a mining operation.

Other systems could be conceived for the future to reduce the number of hazardous and costly stages involved in the mining operation: gathering the nodules, lifting them to the mining ship, transferring them to an ore carrier, transporting them to the processing plant which may be several thousand miles away, processing the metals, and disposing of the tailings. One could, for instance, imagine a system that gathers the nodules on the seabed, loads them on submarines, and transports them directly to the processing plant, thus eliminating the extremely difficult and costly step of lifting them. One might even question the rationale of lifting, say, three million tons of nodules from a depth of five thousand meters and transporting them over thousands of miles, only to extract ninety thousand tons of useful metals and dump almost three million tons. It would seem more rational to collect this mass of nodules on the seabed, process them there in a fully automated, closed system— most likely through a bioindustrial process utilizing bacteria to extract the useful metals—and load the metals on submarines.

These nodules are incredibly abundant. There are literally trillions of them in the Central Pacific alone, and, even assuming that for various technical reasons only 1 percent is commercially recoverable, the reserve is such that it would satisfy demand for thousands of years.

Nodule mining technology has been adapted to the mining of metalliferous muds from the bottom of the Red Sea. It can be adapted as well to the mining of the polymetallic sulphides and cobalt and manganese crusts.

Economic recession, the overabundance of land-based resources, and the instability of prices have slowed down exploration, research, and development in ocean mining in recent years. In the long term, however, ocean mining offers a number of advantages over land-based mining. First, it avoids conflict with competing land uses such as agriculture, grazing, or human habitat. Second, mountain mining has been throughout history, and still is, a hazardous and demeaning occupation, reserved, until not too long ago, for slaves and criminals. Ocean mining is a high-technology undertaking, involving far less manual drudgery and danger to health and life. Third, the environmental impact of ocean mining on human habitat is less than that of land-based mining, although the impact of the former on the marine environment may be great and a number of problems must be solved before ocean mining can become commercial on a large scale. A problem that arises in connection with nodule mining as well as with mining metalliferous muds is that only about 3 percent of the mined material is useful. The remaining 97 percent is waste that must be disposed of in some way. It has been calculated that one individual mining venture, which would process about three million tons of nodules annually for twenty to twenty-five years, would create a wasteland of forty hectares per year—a wasteland of one thousand hectares of chemically poisoned rubble during its lifetime!

Dumping at sea would cause other, until now, unresolved problems, leading one to believe that the undersea harvesting concept described above might offer the only practical solution.

The crucial advantage of ocean mining is that it may be cheaper than land mining. In Southeast Asia, the production costs of offshore tin mining have been estimated to be about 30 percent below the costs of land mining. According to still more optimistic Soviet calculations, offshore mining costs only one-half to one-fifth of mining on land. *Science,* the prestigious journal of the American Association for the Advancement of Science, has reported that, compared with land mining where $9 of capital may produce $1 a year, ocean mining returns $3 for every $1 of capital. Finally, a study on a Cost Model for Ocean Mining by the Massachusetts Institute of Technology has predicted a rate of return of 15–22 percent from ocean mining, which certainly should make it attractive to companies.

If these are sound estimates, then ocean mining will displace land mining in the future. However, this development is bound to generate quite a few social and political displacements, both within and between states.

The industrial revolution can be divided into three phases. The first phase, lasting roughly from the eighteenth century to World War I, was based on coal and steel; the second, from the 1920s through the 1970s, was based on the oil economy; and the third, just beginning, is based on microelectronics, the information and communication revolution, bioindustry, lasers, and space and deep-sea technology. The marine revolution is thus part of the third phase of the industrial revolution (Alvin Toffler's "Third Wave").

The hardships and displacements caused by the first phase—with the proletarization of the masses, culminating in socialist revolutions—are well known. They affected primarily the industrialized countries, with spin-offs in the colonies. The social consequences of the second phase are not yet as well studied and documented, but they are likely to be no less pervasive. They affected, primarily and most painfully, the developing countries—both oil producers and oil importers.

Power derived from oil royalties cannot be conducive to development as they are neither the product of indigenous labor nor the result of development of local productive capacities, but financial assets that are "rentier" in character. The unprecedented influx of labor from nonproducing to producing countries entails social hardships, such as the breakup of family, social structures, and traditions and the growth of slum and squatter settlements. The oil economy tends to create unbearable disequilibria and to encourage the neglect of other vital sectors of the economy. Some oil countries (Libya, Nigeria, Mexico) have permitted their agricultural sector to collapse and have become dependent on imported food. Inflation—worldwide, and generated by the interaction of numerous factors, most important among them, the arms race—has certainly been fomented by spiraling oil prices as well. These have then contributed to the general trend of our time of making the rich richer and the poor poorer and of increasing tension and conflict.

It may be too soon to assess the long-term social and political implications, national and international, of the second phase of the industrial revolution. What is certain is that they are heavy.

The third phase, including the marine revolution, directly affects developed and developing countries as well as the structure of their interrelations. And it is within this context that the impact of a possible shift from land-based mining to ocean mining should be considered.

The displacement of miners, both within the industrialized and the developing countries, while undoubtedly desirable in the long term, may contribute to unemployment in the short term. Miners' unions are powerful, and they will resist ocean mining which is a real threat to their existence. Social tension and political problems of all sorts may be foreseen.

Internationally, the decades since the political emancipation of the former colonies after World War II have been characterized by what might be called a postcolonial extraction economy. That is, the economies of the new nations have been geared not so much to internal development as to the earning of foreign exchange through exporting commodities to the former colonial powers and importing manufactured goods from them. This pattern is, however, breaking down under the impact of the third phase of the industrial revolution. If sugar, cocoa, and coffee are produced through genetic engineering and if metals and minerals are mined from the oceans, they will no longer be imported from the former colonies. While this, again, may be a long-term blessing, permitting at long last a diversification of their economies conducive to internal development, it will undoubtedly also create short-term problems such as the loss of foreign exchange earnings which, in some cases, make up 85–95 percent of the GNP of developing countries.

The measures presently contemplated by the international community to alleviate this problem, particularly in the context of the Law of the Sea negotiations and the work of the Preparatory Commission in Jamaica, are quite inadequate. In accordance with the Convention on the Law of the Sea, these measures are of three kinds: (1) a limitation on the mining production of the International Sea-Bed Authority, (2) compensation to land-based producer countries for export losses arising from production in the international area, and (3) commodity agreements.

The production limitation formula, which the Convention imposes on the International Sea-Bed Authority, is based on projected nickel demand, and it was a bad mistake. If it could have worked at all, it would have protected nickel producers, not producers of cobalt and manganese. It is the latter among developing countries who would suffer most from the displacement. But even if the Authority's production of cobalt and manganese were limited, this would not protect the land-based producers. Contrary to the assumption on which the Convention is based—that the International Sea-Bed Authority would have a monopoly on the mining of nodules—ocean mining will be carried out in areas under national jurisdiction. Thus if there is no limitation on the production of coastal states, the plight of the land-based producers of the same metals and minerals mined from the oceans remains undiminished.

The same problem arises with regard to compensation. The Authority can pay compensation only for losses arising as a consequence of ocean mining in the international area. If mining is carried out in areas under national jurisdiction, there is no compensation. The provisions of the Convention become meaningless in the present context.

Comprehensive commodity agreements appear to be the most promising of the three "remedies." However, they are effective only under certain limited circumstances involving a few homogeneous producers. They have been relatively successful in the case of copper, but whether they would work in the case of nickel, cobalt, and manganese is an open question.

Although the economic effects of ocean mining are some decades away, it is essential to start planning for them now. This can be done through the Preparatory Commission, which has established a special commission to consider this problem. Two approaches seem practical.

In the first approach, immediate, practical steps should be taken toward diversification of the economies of land-based producers to lessen their dependence on export earnings from cobalt and manganese. The pioneers among ocean miners, who under the new Law of the Sea already have certain obligations with respect to the Authority and to developing countries (training of personnel, transfer of technology, exploration of mine sites for the Authority), should be encouraged to assist in this process of diversification through the establishment of mutually advantageous joint ventures in various appropriate industries geared to internal development in such countries. A revolving fund might be established, based on principles similar to those on which the United Nations Revolving Fund for the Exploration of Hard Minerals and Geothermal Energy in Developing Countries is based. We shall return to this in Chapter 3.

The second approach is to encourage land-based producer countries to participate in ocean mining enterprises and to take advantage of their land mining infrastructures, especially in the processing sector, wherever practical. Feasibility studies for land-based producer countries should be undertaken as soon as possible.

Long-term benefits and short-term hardships thus appear to be the key phrases in describing the impact of the impending shift from land-based mining to ocean mining in the wider context of the third phase of the industrial revolution. It should be noted, however, that the long-term benefits may remain illusory if the shock of the short-term hardships disrupts the whole system. To alleviate this shock, steps must be taken now, even though these short-term effects may be 15–20 years away. Since the suggested steps are, in any case, in line with the goals of a new international economic order, there are no risks involved in taking them, even if one wanted to assume that the future of ocean mining is as yet uncertain.

Ocean mining is upon us for all the reasons enumerated in these pages; yet in an even wider context this development is of fundamental importance in anthropological terms, just as the emergence of aquaculture.

Oversimplifying a much more complex story, one might say that the early agricultural phase of human existence was one of harmony with nature, based on an economy of renewable resources—that is, a cyclical process of taking from the earth and giving back to the earth.

The industrial revolution broke this harmony. It was, basically, an extractive economy, founded on the extraction of what, until now, were considered to be nonrenewable resources, and increasingly wasteful use of these resources. This resulted in an end product of pollution and the overexploiting and wounding of nature, as the late Aurelio Peccei put it.

A shift to ocean mining might contribute to restoring the balance by taking from the oceans and giving back to the oceans and thereby recycling matter that need no longer be considered nonrenewable.

Energy

The third major aspect of the marine revolution, which is closely linked to the second one, is a shift from reliance on nonrenewable, polluting land-based energy resources to increasing utilization of renewable, nonpolluting ocean energy resources and technologies.

Energy production and mineral production—and, for that matter, energy production and food production—are closely linked. That is, if there were an inexhaustible supply of reasonably priced, nonpolluting energy resources, minerals and metals would also be an inexhaustible resource. Theoretically, such an inexhaustible supply of nonpolluting energy resources does, in fact, exist in the oceans.

As seen in the Appendix, the potential is simply mind-boggling. The power of the tides has been variously estimated as between 300 and 450 terawatts per year (one terawatt equals one thousand gigawatts or one million megawatts).

This power, or a modest part of it, can be extracted in various ways. The most successful tidal power plant to date is the Saint-Malo plant at the mouth of the Rance River in northern France. Built in 1969, this plant generates electricity both when the tide rushes in and when it goes out. About 0.5 million kilowatts are generated each time, or about 500 gigawatts per year. A number of other plants have been built in recent years or are under construction. In Canada, for example, the Bay of Fundy tidal power plant should be completed in the near future, and the Chinese have developed a smaller-scale type of plant, which appears to be economical.

Global electrical energy needs in the early twenty-first century are estimated at about thirty million megawatts or thirty terawatts per hour per annum. According to the most conservative estimates, tidal power alone could provide 300 terawatts on a global basis. Thus in theory it would be possible to satisfy this demand entirely with tidal energy.

Although research on wave power has been going on over several decades, another twenty years of intensive research and development may be required before the exploitation of this potentially great energy source can be carried out on a fully commercial scale.

Along the Atlantic shore of Great Britain, the potential of wave power is such that it could, in theory, satisfy Britain's total electric power requirements, if a shore length of 100 kilometers were exploited at an efficiency of 30 percent.

Ocean currents are another potential energy source. The Gulf Stream, for instance, carries about thirty million cubic meters of water per second past Miami, or more than five times the total flow of all freshwater rivers of the planet put together!

The flow is slow, however—less than a meter per second on the average. Thus while the total energy of the current passing Miami has been estimated to be about twenty-five gigawatts, perhaps 4 percent of this could actually be extracted by an array of low-pressure turbines. They could, nevertheless, produce about 1,000 million watts on a twenty-four-hour basis, or as much as two large nuclear plants, according to the designers of the turbines.

Algae constitute the fastest-growing biomass on earth. Giant kelp grows at a rate of three meters per day, and chlorella, a tiny green alga, doubles every day. Impressive amounts of energy could be extracted from this inexhaustible resource using anaerobic fermentation, which produces methane. Aquatic plants can be used far more efficiently in the process than terrestrial plants due to the much lower lignin content of their cellulose.

According to Dr. Wilcox, an energy farm of 100,000 acres would yield enough energy and other products to sustain about 50,000 persons at today's U.S. per capita consumption levels, or up to 300,000 persons at today's world average per capita consumption level. As specified by this design, farm products would consist of feed for fish and livestock as well as food for humans, methane gas, fertilizers, ethanol, lubricants, waxes, plastic, and fiber—in other words, a complete spectrum of useful petrochemical-type products.

One of the most advanced systems technically, and closest to the realization of commercial production, is Ocean Thermal Energy Conversion (OTEC). An OTEC plant utilizes the temperature differential between cold bottom water and warmer, sunlit surface water to produce low-pressure steam which drives a turbine to generate electricity. This process was invented by Frenchman George Glaude in 1928. Recently, pilot plants have been built off Hawaii by the Americans and off the Pacific island of Nauru by the Japanese. Both plants produce more energy than they consume. By the end of the century, it is expected that a large OTEC plant may produce as much as ten thousand megawatts of power.

OTEC as well as small-scale wave power installations may make a major contribution to changing the development patterns of small islands in tropical waters. These islands frequently lack land-based resources and depend on imported oil. Thus introduction of OTEC would make them energy-independent and would give a boost to agricultural and industrial development.

The most stunning energy potential in the oceans, however, is that of salinity gradients. Only recently given serious consideration by marine technologists, this method of extracting energy from the sea is based, like OTEC, on a very simple scientific principle that exploits the osmotic pressure generated by the contact between less salty and more salty water. In a study published by *Science,* Isaacs and Schmitt[4] calculated that the salinity energy density of a river with respect to the sea is equivalent to the energy density of a 2,400-meter high dam. "Where large rivers flow into the sea, salinity gradient energy is renewable and its utilization at very low efficiencies is defensible—in the Congo, for instance, the full power released in dilution is about 100,000 megawatts."

The salinity energy density of seawater with respect to a coastal brine pond is equivalent to the energy density of a dam three thousand meters high, and salt domes in coastal regions, which often contain petroleum, contain two or three orders of magnitude more energy in the form of latent salinity power than the oil they might contain. Isaacs and Schmitt conclude: "Only the natural fluxes of salinity

41

and temperature gradients could provide energy in excess of the estimated 21st century levels of electric power consumption."

How fast these vast potentials will be realized is a question that is more economic than technological in nature. High petroleum prices encourage investments in research on alternative energy resources. Low petroleum prices—and, obviously, economic depression—discourage such investments. There can be no doubt, however, that sooner or later the petroleum age will end. It is likely, indeed, that we are moving into an area of far more diversified energy resources and far more decentralized energy systems. In these systems, ocean energy is bound to play a major role.

THREE

The Economics of
The Common Heritage

At the heart of the marine revolution and the new order for the oceans is the concept of the common heritage of mankind.

In proposing this concept to the First Committee of the General Assembly in his historic address of November 1, 1967, Ambassador Pardo of Malta chose not to elaborate on the legal and economic content of the concept at that time. The content of the common heritage of mankind as a legal norm must be defined not by the individual state but by the international community, he said on a later occasion.[5]

As finally embodied in the United Nations Convention on the Law of the Sea (1982), the concept has five implications.

The first implication is nonappropriability—that is, the common heritage can be used but not owned. It is an area where there is no property.

Second, it is a system of management in which all users share.

Third, it constitutes an active sharing of not only financial benefits but also the benefits derived from shared management and transfer of technologies. The second and third points change the structural relationship between rich and poor nations and traditional concepts of development aid.

Fourth, the concept of the common heritage implies reservation of ocean space for peaceful purposes.

Fifth, it implies reservation for future generations.

This chapter describes how the concept of the common heritage could well become the nucleus of a new economic theory, applicable not only to the oceans but also to a new economic order in general. The oceans are a great laboratory for establishing a new order. If they encourage new thinking among scientists, technologists, lawyers, experts in international institutions, and ideologists, it is not surprising that the same should apply to economists.

This analysis of the economics of the common heritage is based on a 1980 Report to the Club of Rome, *Dialogue on Wealth and Welfare,* by Orio Giarini. This report is a response to the challenge of our time which, according to Aurelio Peccei as stated in the preface, "demands not only a fresh, diverse concept of ourselves and our world, and of our place and responsibility in it, but also a vision of our economy, as new and revolutionary as the Einstein cosmology was in comparison with the Newtonian concept."[6]

Giarini starts from the incontestable assertion that neither the neoclassic nor the neo-Marxist nor the Keynesian school of economic thought offers tools adequate for analyzing the present economic situation, let alone for solving its problems. The economics of the last three centuries, he points out, is essentially the economics of the first phase of the industrial revolution of Western Europe—"the discipline of industrialization"—and is deeply rooted in Western philosophical thought and its value system. In a world that has moved on to a new, basically different phase of the industrial revolution and in which Western thought has lost its preponderant infuence, this type of economics has little to offer.

Giarini also states that the world is now less and less the extension of a one-sided, "universal" (essentially Europocentric) culture or power. Rather, it is a global, interacting system which will inevitably produce a new culture and, consequently, a new economics.

Three Basic Concepts of Giarini's Theory

Deducted Value

To be more specific, an economic system that destroys its own resources destroys itself. The "added value" it produces as a measure of the GNP is misleading, since much of this added value is, in reality, negative. It is a "deducted value." Workers employed in the manufacture of antipollution devices, for example, add to the GNP, but they do not add to the real wealth of a nation since they are merely compensating for damage done earlier.

In the long term, physical dependence on nonrenewable resources is an untenable economic proposition.

Dowry and Patrimony

Giarini proposes a new concept of wealth and welfare and a new measure for economic value that comprises GNP and capital, but is far more comprehensive. Termed "dowry and patrimony" (D&P), this measure includes a "stock" of goods and services comprising natural (living and nonliving) as well as man-made (material and nonmaterial) goods and services. Rather than restricting itself to the monetarized sector, as the economics of the industrial revolution had to do (which, incidentally, coincides with and is linked to the formation of the modern nation-state), Giarini's economics covers the whole spectrum of monetarized and nonmonetarized activities and deals with the dynamic interactions between them. His theory represents "a new discipline of welfare derived from the synthesis of economics and ecology."[6]

In making two further points about D&P, Giarini says that, first, unlike GNP "the concept of D&P cannot be reduced even with the best will, to a specific nation-state dimension: national histories and traditions as well as resources of any kind coincide only very partially with existing political institutions."[6] The economics of industrialization and of the monetarized sector, as well as the concept of the nation-state, are all going through the same process of transformation.

Second, he states that D&P is not a fixed or given quantity. Rather, it is in a state of dynamic equilibrium, determined by the interaction of its manifold components. Wealth and welfare, based on an optimization of D&P, are a product of resources, capital, and labor in the most comprehensive sense. The optimum balance between the amount of labor, technology, and capital varies according to various constraints. "D&P is never really 'fixed'," Giarini observes. "All its components are continuously subject to a process of accumulation and depletion. To better grasp this reality, we must view it dynamically and not just as a photographic image."[6] His dynamic concept of D&P postulates a shift from an analytical, linear, or causal approach to economics, to a systemic approach. This is not just a matter of theoretical debate. It reflects change in the real situation, with its feedbacks, where all action is continuously modified by its effects, and where each element has a different behavior (inertia) in time.

Utilization Value
The third key concept of Giarini's economic edifice is utilization value. The traditional concept of value—that is, the "exchange value" of a good or service—is not applicable in his system and in the world in which we live, for it is based on the cost of resources and labor to the moment the product is completed and ready for exchange. It does not include deducted value, nor does it include the cost of disposal for waste and the recycling of usable parts. "The real value in all this system is not the *production* value of the final product because *the real final product* of the entire process of production *is a total amount of waste*. What counts and what has *value*, is the *period of utilization* of the products and services: this is the positive part of the balance sheet. . . . The economic problem, then, is not to optimize merely the cost of production but rather to optimize the total utili-

zation value."[6] In this regard, Giarini notes that the cost of waste disposal is rapidly rising, and that "the possibility of converting waste into a usable 'by-product' is gradually diminishing. Specialization is also restricting the adaptability of waste utilization."[6]

The sectoralized free enterprise system, where each economic enterprise aims at maximizing profits in its own sector, and letting the devil take the hindmost, is in fact incompatible with rational use of resources, optimization of utilization value, and maximization of recycling and waste utilization. These goals require a systemic approach, aimed at increasing D&P and public welfare as a whole. Polycultures, which as used in aquaculture reconstruct whole ecosystems where one species feeds on the waste of another and every ecological niche is utilized, are needed for industry as well. That is, factory linkages are needed, planned and integrated in such a way that one feeds on the waste of the other. This is not possible, however, under a classic free enterprise system.

This system frustrates not only the rational use of resources, it also frustrates the rational use of technology.

Among the pathologies of the present system, Giarini mentions "gigantism," or a trend toward larger, ever more complex technology (e.g., nuclear plants, oil rigs, supertankers, and containers). On the one hand, these technologies require huge investments (billions of dollars each), which changes the relationship between the productive or private sector and financial institutions and, ultimately, the state. On the other hand, these technologies affect the nature of the insurance and counter-insurance business. Statistics show, Giarini points out, "that the decrease in the number of accidents (frequency), and the increase in the maximum possible levels of loss are an indication that the situation tends essentially to be unmanageable."[6] The new science of risk management is an outgrowth of this pathology and, like pollution economics, it produces deducted value, not real wealth and welfare. The enormity of the risk is a measure of the vulnerability of the whole system.

Giarini also has some penetrating observations about the use of big technology in developing countries. To modernize, developing countries have to buy foreign technology, which requires foreign currency. To acquire foreign currency, production is geared for export, not for domestic needs. This process does not, however, enhance development. To the contrary, the rural population is usually completely left out of it, and the poor get poorer. In the industrialized countries the process has, in fact, been exactly the reverse. They started by producing for their domestic market and then built up international commercial strength with the production that exceeded domestic demand.

The question is not, Giarini states, that of having a chemical plant, but of running the plant to produce products that add to local wealth and welfare. Thus it is a question of the economic system, not of the technology employed. In an integrated system, aiming at an increase in real wealth and welfare, even capital-intensive technology, by raising productivity can contribute to D&P because profits, which are expatriated under the present system, can be invested in other sectors of the economy, generating employment or occupations producing welfare.

Giarini does not analyze the implications of his theory for the concept of ownership, perhaps because he thinks the question irrelevant. Ownership, like sovereignty, is in a process of transformation, if not dissolution. In many respects it has become illusory and irrelevant—a static value. It might, nevertheless, be useful to underline that what has a utilization value is to be utilized and managed, and what has no exchange value need not be owned in the classical Roman law sense. His theory, implicitly, is a theory of nonownership, which is one of the reasons it is the economic theory of the common heritage.

Problem Areas

Based on the three key concepts of D&P, deducted value, and utilization value, Giarini's theory provides new tools for analyzing the basic reasons for the contemporary pervasive economic malaise—reasons that elude the analytic tools of traditional economics, restricted as they are to the monetary segment of the far wider spectrum of economic activities. On the one hand, the traditional theories do not take into account the important contribution of "free" goods such as air, water, and land to the economy. They also do not include in their calculations and projections the so-called "gray" economy, which cuts across the border separating monetarized and nonmonetarized transactions. These transactions range from a housewife's work to undeclared moonlighting jobs to the illicit drug market—a segment that involves hundreds of billions of dollars annually, and perhaps as much as 15 percent of the global GNP.

Nonmonetarized transactions are increasing in volume and scope as the world economic and financial crisis deepens. Thus the December 20, 1983 business page of the *Süddeutsche Zeitung* carried the headline, "Barter on the Upswing in Consequence of Debt Crisis." The German firm Thyssen reported that there was no chance for expanding the market in domestic trade, but that great opportunities were offered by the possibilities of getting into the rapidly expanding barter trade, in line with the already concluded deals of Romanian steel for coffee from Colombia. According to the article, "One has to take reality as it is, when there are only five or six currencies left that are really convertible. In this situation there is only one solution, and that is a return to the primordial form of trade,"[7] termed, in mongrolized Anglo-German, "barter-Geschäft."

On the other hand, traditional economics fails to take into account the nonmonetary roots of the present inflation. Among these, Giarini lists unprecedented growth in production and consumption, overheated by advertising which creates artificial demand and by Keynesianism which wards off cyclical recessions otherwise slowing down growth. He also lists the insane explosion of military spending and the diminishing returns of technology which appears unable to compensate for the overexploitation of the natural resource sector of our D&P. "These nonmonetary factors are the basic roots of worldwide inflation. They have brought within our horizon increasing scarcities of food and raw materials, and environmental problems which can be overcome only by huge investments and rising costs of production."[6] But neither inflation, to finance increases in wages, costs, and prices, nor credit restrictions, such as rising interest rates which not only stop inflation but bring the whole economy to a grinding halt, can solve the problem. Monetary policies alone cannot cope with problems whose roots are nonmonetary.

Searching for Solutions

Giarini is prudent in offering solutions, and, obviously, none could be offered cut and dried and ready for use. He does, however, indicate which policies are apt to insure that the production of added value to GNP will not simply be a transfer from the nonmonetarized to the monetarized sector of the economy and that the real balance between added and deducted values will not be negative.

Regarding the monetarized sector, he suggests that, in the long term, a global monetary system is inevitable, and that it might be approached through regional efforts. He also has a number of suggestions for strengthening the nonmonetarized sector and integrating it beneficially into the economy as a whole. "For future years, the main strategy should be to mobilize capital and D&P jointly. . . . Recognition of the economic relevance of D&P and capital, of the necessity of stimulating their positive, as opposed to their negative synergy might be of help in providing a more soundly based theoretical framework for a world economic policy combining solidarity, cooperation and self-reliance."[6]

The input of the nonmonetarized sector could be strengthened by encouraging the activities of voluntary organizations in, for example, social services, assistance to the elderly, child care and education, and cultural activities. At a time of increasing structural unemployment— Giarini shows that it is practically impossible to create enough "jobs" for the rapidly growing world population— one may have to look for the creation of occupations rather than jobs. This implies a whole new look at the problems of labor and its needs which must be met by other means if wages are not available.

Giarini has little faith in the present system of income tax as a means of redistributing income. Complex and burdensome, this system encourages evasions and the emergence and growth of the "gray" economy. He favors a tax on consumption, which, of course, differs from a sales tax. A sales tax favors the rich and weighs on the poor, while a tax on consumption can be progressive and enhance redistribution of income.

To strengthen the nonmonetarized sector, Giarini suggests that taxes be paid in cash or in in-kind social services. For example, doctors might perform a certain number of operations free for the community instead of paying a tax. And he suggests that the whole tax system be brought closer to the grass roots and decentralized. "Decentralization would provide a remedy to the extent that it led to the creation, closer to the citizen, of civil-service posts occupied on a rotation basis, with everyone becoming a citizen-administrator in turn. Moreover, it could be desirable for wage-earning to be replaced gradually and partially by honorary work."[6]

In a footnote, Giarini refers to three other important aspects or implications of his theory, which, due to lack of space or because they have been covered amply by other authors, he does not deal in greater detail:

51

— Problems and perspectives of collaboration between public and private institutions.

— Regionalization at the continental level and its contribution to a world system (he refers in particular to a world financial system).

— International taxes.[6]

Giarini's Theory Applied to the Oceans

The above summary cannot do justice to the comprehensiveness, historical perspective, and philosophical depth of Giarini's theory. It may suffice, however, as a basis for indicating the fundamental importance that this new approach to economics may hold for the marine economy. The oceans offer a paradigm for the application and further elaboration of Giarini's theory. Only a new economic theory, like the one he attempts, will be able to cope with the problematique of marine economic policy.

There are four major reasons for this. First, it is clear that the marine revolution has brought an unprecedented injection of D&P into the world economy and the economies of states. The oceans cover three-quarters of the world, and the potential represented by aquatic foods, minerals, metals, and energy is astounding. Whether this massive injection of D&P has occurred under national or international jurisdiction will, in the long term, not be as important as it seems today. The question of sovereignty, over the long run, is as irrelevant to economic development as the question of ownership.

Second, the United Nations has declared that the mineral resources of the deep seabed are the common heritage of mankind, and there are some startling similarities between this concept as it has been developed by its principal author, Arvid Pardo, and Giarini's concept of D&P.

Common heritage, Pardo has stressed time and again, "implies freedom of access and use on the part of those taking part in the heritage, but also regulation of use for the purpose of conserving the heritage and avoiding the infringement of the rights of others; inherent in the regulation of use is, of course, the responsibility for misuse. The concept finally implies the equitable distribution of benefits from exploitation of the heritage."[8]

Pardo's concept of common heritage is as comprehensive as Giarini's. It includes not only resources, it also includes values, and scientific research as well.

Similarly, his concept is dynamic like Giarini's. The content of common heritage is "determined pragmatically in relation to felt international needs."[8] It is not limited to a complex of real or potential resources. "World resources," he points out, "should not be conceived in a static sense. . . . New resources are being constantly created by technology."[8] The similarities are striking.

Third, the marine revolution postulates a synthesis between ecology and economy as a precondition for its lasting success. The monitoring of changes in the ocean environment and the surveillance of activities apt to induce such changes are an essential part of any scheme for the management of marine resources. The United Nations Convention on the Law of the Sea, which deals for the first time in history with all major economic uses of the oceans, contains the first ecological framework for the protection and conservation of the marine environment. This framework precisely allocates responsibilities, liabilities, and enforcement procedures. This is indeed one of the most innovative and forward-looking aspects of the Convention, but it was dictated by the very nature of things. The rational use of marine resources is physically impossible without consideration of the marine ecology, including the behavior and movement of living resources and physical and chemical oceanographic conditions.

Fourth, all major economic uses of the oceans interact. A sectoral approach to ocean economics is obsolete and impractical. For example, offshore oil production has an impact on fisheries. Trawling affects the laying of cables and pipelines. Aquaculture developments and the construction of artificial islands and installations may interfere with shipping lanes. Offshore and inshore also interact. The management of ports and harbors, of sea-borne trade, and of tourism are all integral parts of one single ecological system, and changes in any one will induce changes in all others. Finally, multiple uses of single marine technologies have been shown to increase productivity and profitability.

Ocean management must be broadly interdisciplinary if it is to work at all. The very concept of the economic zone embodies this problematique of the oceans. An economic zone is not a fisheries zone, a zone for the protection of the environment, or a dumping or a mineral mining zone. It is a zone for the management of all economic and ecological uses of the sea, considered in their interaction. The same concept is enshrined in the preamble to the Convention, where the signatories state that they are "conscious that the problems of ocean space are closely interrelated and need to be considered as a whole."

For the four reasons outlined above the oceans provide a unique occasion to apply and test Giarini's theory, which may provide a seminal input to the development of the common heritage concept. In legal and constitutional terms, the United Nations Convention on the Law of the Sea pushes developments far in the direction of Giarini's thinking. It is, in fact, ahead of him. The legal and institutional framework—no matter how imperfect in reality—is there, and to this we shall return in the next chapter. The economic content must now be elaborated in the Preparatory Commission and in other fora. It will be a long and difficult process, but Giarini's theories may provide some guidance.

Preparation for the Future

Ocean Mining

As a base strategy, it will be recalled, Giarini recommends mobilizing, for future years, capital and D&P jointly, based on "recognition of the economic relevance of D&P and capital, of the necessity of stimulating their positive, as opposed to their negative synergy, [within a] theoretical framework for a world economic policy combining solidarity, cooperation and self-reliance."[6]

Could there be a more striking, a more concrete, or a more immediately practical example of such a policy than joint, international investment of capital in the utilization of the common heritage of mankind?

The amazing fact is that we are not talking about dreams of an idealized future. The legal, institutional, and operational framework for the enactment of such a policy has been created; it exists and it is operating. We have an interim regime for exploration, research, and development in place in the form of the Preparatory Commission for the International Sea-Bed Authority and the International Tribunal for the Law of the Sea.

The Preparatory Commission was established by a resolution adopted by the Third United Nations Conference on the Law of the Sea (UNCLOS III), together with the Convention. The Commission is composed of all signatories to the Convention (159), as well as a small number of observers—that is, delegations of states who have not signed the Convention but have signed the final act of the Conference.

The task of the Commission is to manage transition in the interim period between the signing of the Convention and its coming into force. The latter requires sixty ratifications and is likely to take a few years.

The Commission is presently studying the modalities of establishing a Joint Venture for Exploration, Research and Development (JEFERAD), first proposed by the delegation of Austria. This undertaking—a new form of industrial-scientific cooperation between North and South—should mobilize investments of $200 million for a five-year period. These investments will be used to engage in exploration for a mine site for the future International Sea-Bed

Authority and to create a technology bank for the future Authority to which private and state companies may, at fair and reasonable commercial prices, cede technology the Authority will need once the Convention comes into force. These investments will also be used to train personnel from developing countries both in the new discipline of wealth and welfare derived from the synthesis of economics and ecology and in the sciences on which marine technology is based.

The exploitation of the resource is, in a way, a secondary goal, and it will take place at least a decade and a half in the future. What is of immediate importance is the joint mobilization of capital and D&P or common heritage—a common heritage comprising resources as well as science and technology and ethical values.

When it comes, the exploitation of resources will not fall into the traditional pattern of exhausting a nonrenewable resource. In the economy/ecology of the oceans, as we have seen, minerals and metals are a continuously renewable resource.

Deducted value will be a factor, and the problem is how to minimize it. It will require careful monitoring of the marine environment, imaginative and constructive processes of waste recycling or minimizing waste through processing on the ocean floor, and realistic and forward-looking measures to protect land-based producers of metals and minerals whose earnings will be adversely affected by ocean mining. Minimization of deducted value cannot be achieved by limiting the production of ocean mining or by paying compensation as presently considered by the Commission. The location in time and in space of commercial-scale ocean mining is too uncertain at present to permit the adoption of precise measures of this kind. If ocean mining is carried out in areas under national as well as international jurisdiction, limitations on and compensation for production in the international area would be meaningless.

It is quite certain, nevertheless, that ocean mining will affect the prices of at least some metals (certainly cobalt and manganese) and will cause displacements. The best way to minimize the harmful effects of these displacements is to use the interim period to plan for alternative earnings—that is, to facilitate the diversification of the economies of those developing countries (e.g., Zambia, Zaire, Zimbabwe) that depend overwhelmingly on the export earnings from one commodity. In Chapter 2, some measures were suggested to cope with this problem, including the establishment of a revolving fund for industrial diversification, in which UNIDO (United Nations Industrial Development Organization), UNCTAD (United Nations Conference on Trade and Development), UNDP (United Nations Development Programme), the World Bank, and the Jamaica Commission would cooperate. Using the precedent set by the United Nations Revolving Fund for the Exploration of Hard Minerals and Geothermal Energy in Developing Countries, the new fund would be financed initially by voluntary contributions. It, in turn, would finance industrial enterprises in the affected land-based producer countries—for example, bioindustries, which have enormous potential for the future, are not highly capital-intensive, and might offer developing countries the opportunity to pass into the most advanced phase of the industrial revolution, without "recapitulating" (and never catching up with) the previous, already obsolete phases.

In return—again following the pattern of the United Nations revolving fund for mineral exploration—countries benefiting from the assistance of the new fund would help replenish its capital by paying 1 percent of the revenues of industries created by the fund once their products come on stream. In the case of the revolving fund for mineral exploration, such payments are made over a period of fifteen years.

The developing land-based producer countries, dependent as they are on earnings from the export of one or two commodities which are of no value for internal consumption, fall into the pattern described above by Giarini. The measure proposed here might go a long way toward redressing this unfortunate course of negative economic development. The liberation of developing countries from the grip of the postcolonial extraction economy may indeed be one of the unheralded by-products of the marine revolution.

Here again, it is not so much the monetary value of the common heritage that matters. In dollars and cents, this value will, for the foreseeable future, be marginal, almost negligible, if measured against the economic needs of development cooperation. It is the concept, as well as the methodology that this concept suggests, that might be instrumental in turning things around.

Aquaculture

As a means of strengthening the nonmonetarized sector of the economy, Giarini suggests the creation of productive occupations rather than jobs—"occupations that produce real value which, however, need not be monetarized but could contribute equally to real wealth and well being."[6] Could there be a more striking example of this kind of economy activity than aquaculture? Aquaculture fully straddles the boundary between the monetarized and the nonmonetarized sector. It includes, on one hand, the capital- and energy-intensive production of luxury items such as prawns or pearls, largely for export. On the other hand, it is undertaken by the small farm (Indonesian or Indian in style), the family farm, or the Chinese-style community farm, where everyone pitches in, but no one is actually a full-time, four-season, paid fish farmer, and production is largely consumed by the family or the village community. The possibilities of expanding this type of activity, as was pointed out in Chapter 2, are enormous. Expansion would then result in an increase in D&P, largely through the valorization of the nonmonetarized sector. This would also serve as a starting point for reversing the absurd postcolonial extraction economy situation in which countries heavily dependent on fish protein for their nutrition let their fish be fished out by foreign fleets and then spend their precious foreign exchange earnings to import canned fish.

Monitoring and Surveillance

Unpaid labor plays an important role in other aspects of ocean management as well. Monitoring of the marine environment and surveillance of activities apt to induce detrimental changes in the environment require the voluntary cooperation of professional scientists, fishermen, mariners, environmental organizations, and concerned citizens. The recent establishment of a self-policing association of Greek shipowners to protect the marine environment in the Mediterranean (HELMEPA) is a good example. Police action, while necessary, cannot entirely solve the problem of enforcement. It must be complemented by voluntary action and self-enforcement. In a recent book, *La sécurité en mer,* Philippe Boisson[9] writes: "It would appear that respect for technical rules and regulations depends essentially on the valor and conscience of seamen. Considering the immensity of the oceans and the difficulties of controlling them, the fear of the policeman remains ineffective."

An outstanding Japanese environmental expert and fighter, Jun Ui[10] of the University of Tokyo, has stressed the need for a "decentralized and self-governing system," in which scientists, grass-roots environmental movements, and concerned citizens monitor and fight not only pollution, but also the interest and pressure groups around the polluting industries which try to block an effective environmental policy—and he used Japan as a striking example. The requirements of ocean management may, again, foster much broader sociopolitical activities (nonmonetary), aiming, in this case, at a structure close to the grass roots and very similar to the one postulated by Giarini.

One aspect of Giarini's theory may need further development. The new emphasis on the nonmonetarized sector, and on unpaid, productive occupations rather than on paid, even though often unproductive jobs, requires more social services, which, in turn, may straddle the monetarized and nonmonetarized sectors. Unquestionably, material incentives such as free housing, food bonuses, life-long scholarships for adult education, or free medical services must be offered to unpaid workers. In a number of oil-producing countries, such measures have already been taken. Doctors, who in Giarini's scheme would have the option of paying their taxes in the form of unpaid services to the community, might be directed to render such services particularly to the unpaid worker. In a decentralized, self-managing socioeconomic system, such procedures become quite practical.

Regional Development

Giarini has high hopes for the success of regional integration, enhanced by a multiplicity of concrete common problems. The establishment of regional unified currencies—as recently undertaken by the states of the Andean region—may be a step toward creation of a world currency, an essential tool for bringing some order into the monetary chaos of our time.

Ocean management requires regional integration more than any other sector of the world economy. It is in fact impossible without regional cooperation and integration. Fish do not recognize the political boundaries of coastal states, nor do pollution, ocean currents, and winds and weather. Oil fields and mineral deposits may straddle boundaries as well. The management of living resources calls for strict regional cooperation among coastal states through international organizations such as the regional fishery commissions, all of which are presently engaged in strengthening and restructuring their activities so that they can respond to the new and increased demands made on them by coastal states. These include demands for assistance in management, manpower training, technology transfer, legislation, and policy coordination.

The protection of the marine environment equally depends on regional integration of policies for ecological as well as for economic reasons. The ecological reasons are obvious. An economic reason is that unilateral anti-pollution measures might put an industry at an economic disadvantage, rendering it noncompetitive. Such measures must therefore be international and enforceable for all the industries in a given region, or they cannot be taken at all.

Marine scientific research, likewise, cannot be conducted successfully on a strictly national basis for ecological as well as economic reasons. Since the ecological system to be researched ignores national boundaries, so must the researcher, and regional arrangements must be made accordingly. Oceanographic research, furthermore, is too expensive to be carried out individually by most nations, especially in regions of developing countries. The cooperative use of oceanographic ships and regional oceanographic institutions is the only solution to this problem.

Fortunately, all of the problems described above are provided for in the United Nations Convention on the Law of the Sea. Moreover, they are being pursued vigorously by the Regional Seas Programme, which was initiated by UNEP (United Nations Environmental Programme) in cooperation with about 110 coastal states; all the U.N. agencies engaged in ocean activities; and a great number of other intergovernmental and nongovernmental organizations.

One can imagine that the regional communality of interests, and the establishment of joint management systems and joint mechanisms for monitoring, surveillance, and enforcement, might generate as a by-product an element of disarmament and arms control. The movement for regional ocean denuclearization is rapidly gaining momentum in the Pacific and Indian oceans and in the Baltic and Mediterranean seas. The same mechanisms established to monitor the ocean environment to assure peaceful uses of the ocean and compliance with rules, standards, and regulations can be used to monitor and enforce arms control and disarmament measures. The machinery is being put into place, and all that is needed is the political will to use it. It is encouraging that the Soviet Union favors such a development.

The fact that the Regional Seas Programme and the related programs of FAO for regional fisheries management and of the Intergovernmental Oceanographic Commission (IOC) for regional cooperation in marine scientific research do not move as rapidly and straightforwardly as pure reason might wish to dictate is natural. There are countercurrents and inertia. Reality moves painfully slowly, and the daily labor of the shaker and mover is beset with continuous frustration. It is only from a longer perspective—perhaps, ten years—that one can measure success or failure, and as Giarini, quoting Tolstoi, notes, changes are perceived when they have already taken place and not when they are under way.

What can already be clearly seen today, roughly a decade after the Exclusive Economic Zone (EEZ) was first conceived, is that the lasting significance of the EEZ is not national aggrandizement—not that it was "the biggest grab in history,"[11] as the late Lord Ritchie Calder called it, commenting on the Caracas session of the United Nations Conference on the Law of the Sea in 1974. Its lasting significance is that it institutionalizes the transition from a laissez-faire system to a system of economic ocean management which, by its very nature and because of the inextricable interactions between its ecological and its economic components, transcends national boundaries and accelerates regional integration. Since this development has to start from the here and now, it is quite logical that it should start from economic zones under national jurisdiction. Nation-states are the basis from which we must work and move forward toward their integration rather than starting from the establishment of strong international institutions for which, in many cases, a realistic basis does not yet exist and which are the end of the process rather than the starting point.

An Ocean Development Tax

With regard to taxes, Giarini sees the need for international taxation and favors a taxation system based on consumption.

This author has, for the past fifteen years, proposed the establishment of an ocean development tax, based on the uses of the oceans.[12] This tax is, in a way, on consumption—that is, on the utilization and consumption of ocean space and resources. This proposal calls for a 1 percent tax (modified by population and GNP) on all the major commercial uses of the ocean—on fish caught, oil extracted, minerals produced, goods and persons shipped, water desalinated, recreation enjoyed, waste dumped, pipelines laid, and installations built. There would be no tax, however, on subsistence fisheries or on scientific research. This tax would be levied on activities no matter where located—in areas under national or international jurisdiction. This functional, not territorial, tax would be levied by governments and paid over to the competent ocean institutions (e.g., FAO, UNEP, IOC, International Maritime Organization [IMO], International Sea-Bed Authority) for the purpose of building and improving ocean services (e.g., navigational aids, scientific infrastructure, environmental monitoring, search and rescue, disaster relief, etc.).

Taxes, as stressed at the time that this tax was initially proposed, must be directly and tangibly linked to useful services; otherwise, nations (or individuals!) will refuse to pay them. Services, on the other hand, cost, and they must be paid for. Thus they must be linked to some form of taxes. To base contributions to ocean institutions on the usual U.N. scale of contributions seemed rather meaningless as it lacked any tangible links with the use countries make of the oceans and what they get out of them. The proposed system would be flexible and decentralized among the few global ocean institutions and regional systems providing services.

The Regional Seas Programme has indeed already begun with the establishment of regional funds to pay for the services it is to provide. The establishment of an ocean development tax would strengthen these funds. It might also contribute to the creation of regional monetary systems or currencies.

This proposal was hailed, in 1971, as "an extremely important, interesting suggestion, and perhaps a very promising proposal" by Ambassador Jorge Castañeda of Mexico (later, foreign minister of Mexico).[13] He observed that "if we act intelligently, it has a fair chance of becoming a reality in the near future."

J. Alan Beesley of Canada said: "Lawyers feel they must solve the problems they are facing now. We must, in 1973 [when the Law of the Sea Conference was to start] try to solve problems we are going to face in the future. And if we think of the problems of the future, this very radical and revolutionary idea of an ocean development tax is not nearly as futuristic and academic as it now might seem to be."[14]

And Silviu Brucan of Romania observed: "It is in my opinion one of those new daring proposals that is bound to gain ground in international life because it is based on the progressive forces at work in world politics and rides the wave of the future."[15]

Beesley and the Canadian government pursued the idea at some length in the Committee on the Peaceful Uses of the Sea-bed, the Ocean Floor and the Subsoil thereof Beyond the Limits of National Jurisdiction, 1968-1973. He introduced the proposal in the committee in March 1971, and suggested that states

> begin to pay over to the interim international machinery [the seabed committee] a fixed percentage of all the reve-

nue they derive from the whole of the sea-bed area claimed by them beyond the outer limit of their internal waters. One percent of such revenues, for example, could produce many millions of dollars for the benefit of the international community and the developing countries in particular, as much as 15 million dollars a month, according to some sources. The revenues from the coastal State would constitute a sort of "voluntary international development tax" to be paid over in the period pending the adoption of a multilateral treaty on the limits of national jurisdiction and the creation of an international regime for the sea-bed beyond national jurisdiction.

I realize that this suggested . . . step is radical and even revolutionary in nature. The Government of Canada for its part would be prepared to take it.[14]

While his official proposal was restricted to the mineral resources of the continental shelf, he pointed out that "a different range of issues would be raised by that second possibility which we are in fact prepared to discuss, but there is no Canadian governmental position on the imposition of an ocean development tax on the living resources of the sea. This is another question we are considering."[14] The proposal died a quick death in the committee, but its spirit lived on.

During UNCLOS III, the delegation of Nepal introduced a similar proposal—again, restricted to nonliving resources—for a tax to be paid to a Common Heritage Fund. This fund would have contributed to compensating for the inequities inherent in the establishment of the EEZ, which gives too much to a few states—mostly rich—and so little or nothing to many others, the poorest among them. The Nepalese proposal gathered respectable support: cosponsorship by thirteen states and support from many others. But it too died. Perhaps the timing was unfortunate—as so many good ideas, they come either too early or too late. When the Nepalese proposal finally came to the floor in 1981, it was too late for innovations or major changes to be made in the draft Convention.

The moment for the ocean development tax may come—must come—after the Convention has come into force. At that time, the tax could be introduced as an additional optional protocol, linked to specific services to be rendered by specified ocean institutions. An ocean development tax that generates a few billion dollars in international revenue, whether in currency or in ocean management services, would go a long way in compensating for the inequities inevitably inherent in the present EEZ allocations. It could also carry us beyond the present, somewhat colonial, or postcolonial or neocolonial, trend of dividing the common heritage to the advantage of the "have" and to the detriment of the "have-not" states. Such a tax would embody one of the basic concepts of the economics of the common heritage.

Work for the Future
The management and conservation of marine resources (both living and nonliving), the marine environment, and the related marine sciences, technologies, and services, constitute the most important addition to "dowry and patrimony" in the history of economics. Thus development of the economics of the common heritage, including the establishment of appropriate infrastructures, could significantly foster further development of the economics of D&P. A great deal of research will be needed in this new field on, for example, the need for and the cost of subregional, national, regional, and global services and the effective management of the marine environment and its resources, and the monetary and nonmonetary inputs into these services. Research will also be needed on deducted values arising from negative synergisms of conflicting uses of ocean space and resources; from present technological gigantism, risk management, and pollution economics; and from conflicts between military and peaceful uses of the marine sector of the economy. In addition, investigators must examine the utilization value of services provided and

production created (for example, by aquaculture facilities and technologies, mining ships and technologies, and OTEC plants); the generation of secondary and subsidiary industries (e.g., canning, construction, pharmaceuticals, petrochemicals, land-based transportation); and above all, how to define a set of usable social indicators that will properly assess and monitor the generation of real wealth. The latter research need would help point out inadequate economic policies and organize actions toward specific as well as general goals. It should be a feasible exercise to select the most adequate indicators, even considering the delicate political problems likely to be encountered in gaining their acceptance. A recognized institute could then issue periodic verifications of the changes brought about in the level of wealth, with reference to the indicators, and stimulate the appropriate actions.

Obviously, much of this material exists, and all that must be done is to reorganize and recast it in the context of the new theory. While further developing and refining the economics of the common heritage, such a work would also provide guidelines for the implementation of badly needed ocean economic policies.

For reasons of political expediency and realism, the concept of the common heritage of mankind was first embodied and institutionalized in the very restricted sector of the almost mythical manganese nodules. In spite of strong counterpressures and inertia, the concept is rapidly expanding to embrace all marine resources and services, whether we call them by the name of common heritage or not. Thus Shigeru Oda of the International Court of Justice recently wrote:

> Meanwhile, with regard to sea-bed mineral resources, a new international regime of the deep ocean floor has been emerging from the discussions of UNCLOS III for international control of these resources based upon the basic concept of the common heritage of mankind. Who can say that the same trend will not be followed in regard to ocean

fishing? Surely, discussions similar to those now taking place on sea-bed mineral resources will eventually be held on the new concept of the common heritage of mankind as applicable to ocean fishing.[16]

Outer space and the moon and its resources have already been declared to be the common heritage of mankind, and if and when technology advances sufficiently to make these resources economically interesting, a machinery will have to be established to manage them. Antarctica will follow (the proposal has already been tabled by Malaysia in the General Assembly of the United Nations). The ball is rolling and cannot be stopped. Other basic goods and services, like food and energy, will follow, until the concept of the common heritage, with its institutional infrastructure, coincides with that of D&P. We will then have moved to a system of economics, based on new concepts of value and of ownership and sovereignty, as different from traditional economics as Einstein's physics is from Newton's.

FOUR

A Constitution for the Oceans:

Systems-Maintaining

United Nations Convention on the Law of the Sea

PREAMBLE

The States Parties to this Convention,

Prompted by the desire to settle, in a spirit of mutual understanding and co-operation, all issues relating to the law of the sea and aware of the historic significance of this Convention as an important contribution to the maintenance of peace, justice and progress for all peoples of the world,

Noting that developments since the United Nations Conferences on the Law of the Sea held at Geneva in 1958 and 1960 have accentuated the need for a new and generally acceptable Convention on the law of the sea,

Conscious that the problems of ocean space are closely interrelated and need to be considered as a whole,

Recognizing the desirability of establishing through this Convention, with due regard for the sovereignty of all States, a legal order for the seas and oceans which will facilitate international communication, and will promote the peaceful uses of the seas and oceans, the equitable and efficient utilization of their resources, the conservation of their living resources, and the study, protection and preservation of the marine environment,

Bearing in mind that the achievement of these goals will contribute to the realization of a just and equitable international economic order which takes into account the interests and needs of mankind as a whole and, in particular, the special interests and needs of developing countries, whether coastal or land-locked,

Desiring by this Convention to develop the principles embodied in resolution 2749 (XXV) of 17 December 1970 in which the General Assembly of the United Nations solemnly declared *inter alia* that the area of the sea-bed and ocean floor and the subsoil thereof, beyond the limits of national jurisdiction, as well as its resources, are the common heritage of mankind, the exploration and exploitation of which shall be carried out for the benefit of mankind as a whole, irrespective of the geographical location of States,

Believing that the codification and progressive development of the law of the sea achieved in this Convention will contribute to the strengthening of peace, security, cooperation and friendly relations among all nations in conformity with the principles of justice and equal rights and will promote the economic and social advancement of all peoples of the world, in accordance with the Purposes and Principles of the United Nations as set forth in the Charter,

Affirming that matters not regulated by this Convention continue to be governed by the rules and principles of general international law,

Have agreed as follows:

* * *

In this chapter, an analysis of the results of the Third United Nations Conference on the Law of the Sea (1973–1982) is placed in the wider context of the marine revolution and the emergence of the economics of the common heritage. Specifically, attention is focused on the future: How will the new ocean regime work? What will be the consequences? What will it contribute to building a new international order?

The history of the Conference and the contents of the Convention have been summarized and analyzed hundreds of times in hundreds of places by "insiders"—that is, those of us who had the privilege of participating in the Conference as actors in the drama—as well as outside critics, academicians, and politicians.

Some have taken a dim, even cynical, view of UNCLOS III and the Convention. Nationalism triumphed, as they see it. A great dream has been debased and betrayed, and a unique opportunity has been missed. The result is a Convention that is nonviable and full of gaps, ambiguities, and contradictions. Whether the Convention will ever obtain the required number of ratifications (sixty) is immaterial, for even if it came into force, it would be powerless in the face of further escalations of national claims, generating conflict and pollution and frustrating conservation of living resources and marine scientific research. The International Sea-Bed Authority, in the eyes of these critics, is a creature stillborn—ill-conceived under assumptions remote from reality and crushed prenatally by the weight of unwieldy international bureaucracies.

Even the critics and cynics, however, concede that UNCLOS III has been a unique historic development, creating precedents as terrifying to them as they are inspiring to those seeking a new international order.

The concept of the oceans, and particularly the seabed, as a common heritage had been formulated previously by

71

French jurists and others. However, this concept remained in academia or in the realm of rhetoric. The man who brought it down to earth and into the arena of world politics was Arvid Pardo, the ambassador from Malta, in his historic address to the United Nations General Assembly of November 1, 1967. He placed the concept in the full context of technological, economic, and political developments. These developments included the penetration of the industrial revolution into the oceans, the escalation of national claims to enclose as much as possible of the oceans' newly discovered wealth, and the collapse of the old order based on the freedom of the seas. They also included the need for a new order that would ensure freedom of navigation, cope rationally with the problems of pollution and overfishing, halt the trend toward expansion of national claims, and utilize the no-man's-land of the deep seabed beyond the limits of national jurisdiction for a new beginning.

With astonishing precision Arvid Pardo indicated every step on the long road that should lead from the then and there to the realization of his vision: the appointment of an ad hoc committee to study the question in depth, the adoption of a declaration of principles setting forth the new concept, the calling of the Third United Nations Conference on the Law of the Sea, and the adoption of a universally acceptable convention embodying the new order. Thus Pardo displayed a rare combination of vision and strategy, utopianism and realism, and perception of national and economic interests and idealism. And it is only when the latter two drives—economic self-interest and idealism—coincide that mankind gets on the move. Then nothing is stronger than a great idea whose time has come.

The international community followed suit. An ad hoc committee was appointed to study the question. A declaration of principles was adopted in 1970, together with two other resolutions. One declared the 1970s to be the first international decade of ocean exploration, while the other declared a moratorium on unilateral seabed mining prior to the establishment of an international regime. The principle of reservation of the seabed for peaceful purposes was enshrined in 1971 in the Treaty (however defective) on the Prohibition of the Emplacement of Nuclear Weapons and Other Weapons of Mass Destruction on the Sea-Bed and the Ocean Floor and in the Subsoil Thereof. In 1973, a comprehensive agenda was adopted for UNCLOS III, which got under way in December 1973 for a brief procedural session, followed by the first long working session in Caracas, Venezuela, in the summer of 1974. The work to be done was without precedent.

In truth, the law of the sea was no longer the law of the sea. The traditional law of the sea was a tidy compartment of international law for the experts to handle, but the penetration of the industrial revolution into the oceans had completely and irreversibly transformed it. A convention dealing with all major uses of the seas was therefore no longer a convention on the law of the sea. Without being aware of it, a huge world constituent assembly had gathered in Caracas to lay the cornerstone of a new international economic order and write a constitution for the oceans that had to be a constitution for the world. Thus it is no wonder that the process took ten years and that the assembly was the largest and longest international assembly in history.

The Convention, as it finally emerged, is not Plato's Republic or More's Utopia. It is not a philosophical treatise or a blueprint for perfection. It is a political compromise reflecting antagonistic and often irreconcilable trends and aspirations among states and within states, between coastal (resource-oriented) interests and shipping interests, between commodity producers and commodity consumers, between "haves" and "have-nots," between advocates of free enterprise and believers in a planned economy, between traditionalists/conservatives and innovators, and between the past and the future. It is a document of transition and of unfinished business, which, in a way, can never be finished because perfection is not of this earth. It has, however, given an impetus without precedent to a process which is now on course in a new direction. This process is itself rewarding in the sense of the French philosopher Albert Camus who said, paraphrasing Lao-tse, that the goal is the way; the way is the goal.

Organization of the Convention

The 320 articles of the Convention itself (followed by nine technical annexes) are divided into seventeen parts.

Parts I–X update and codify the traditional law of the sea. They set boundaries, define areas of jurisdiction, and basically cover the traditional uses of the sea, fishing and navigation. In a sense they constitute the "systems-maintaining" part of the Convention. They are conservative, and they satisfy the Superpowers' basic perceived needs: sovereign rights over oil exploration and exploitation on the outer continental shelf; a fisheries conservation zone; and untrammelled passage through international straits for all ships, including warships and submarines. These were in fact the issues the Superpowers tried to negotiate in the 1960s and which induced them to favor the calling of UNCLOS III in 1973.

The industrialized coastal states and the great maritime powers definitely have more to gain from Parts I–X than the developing countries, although the latter have made important contributions and, in the long term, may also gain.

Part I of the Convention merely introduces and defines a few technical terms, which it does rather randomly and scantily. In fact, only six terms are defined: the "Area" of the international seabed, the "Authority" established to manage the resources of the Area, "activities in the Area," "pollution of the marine environment," "dumping," and "States Parties" to the Convention. One wonders why just these are defined, thereby excluding a great many other new terms introduced in the Convention. This part should have been dropped altogether or it should have been developed more fully.

Part II defines the territorial sea and the contiguous zone in terms almost identical to those of the 1958 Convention on the Territorial Sea and the Contiguous Zone, except that the limit of the territorial sea is now agreed to be at twelve nautical miles from the baselines, whereas no agreement had been reached on this limit either in 1958 at UNCLOS I or in 1960 at UNCLOS II. It is curious how an issue that could not be solved in the earlier context caused very little discussion in the new context, permitting a solution that was universally acceptable.

"Innocent passage," which, as in the 1958 Convention, is to be enjoyed by all ships in the territorial sea, is far more carefully defined than in the earlier Convention. It is still subject to suspension under certain circumstances, and submarines are obliged to navigate on the surface and show their flag.

The definition of the contiguous zone, again, resumes the language of the 1958 Convention, except that in the 1958 Convention the seaward limit was defined as twelve miles from the baselines, whereas in the new Convention it is twenty-four nautical miles.

Part III is the price that the coastal states pay for the extension of the territorial sea granted them in Part II. This is the new concept of "transit passage" through straits used for international navigation. This passage cannot be suspended under any circumstances, and ships may navigate in their "normal mode." In the case of submarines, this means submerged.

Thus between Parts II and III the major interests of the coastal and maritime states are ably and fairly balanced and harmonized. It is this kind of "package deal," based on a new understanding of the interdependence of issues (in this case, the expansion of the territorial sea and the question of passage through straits), that permitted the solution of problems that eluded the earlier conference.

Part IV introduces another new concept: the archipelagic state—that is, a state consisting of a group of islands, "including parts of islands, interconnecting waters and other natural features which are so closely interrelated that such islands, waters and other natural features form an intrinsic geographical, economic and political entity, or which historically have been regarded as such." This category includes states such as Indonesia, Fiji, or the Philippines, which have fought for recognition of this principle for a long time as an essential means of strengthening their national unity.

One of the qualifications of an archipelagic state is that the ratio between the land areas (the aggregate area of all the component islands) and the archipelagic waters (the water enclosed by baselines joining the outermost points of the outermost islands and drying reefs) may not exceed one to nine. Considering that a territorial sea, contiguous zone, economic zone, etc., are measured outward from these baselines enclosing the archipelagic waters, it is clear that the expansion of ocean space falling under the jurisdiction of archipelagic states is enormous. This may result in problems of control and management for archipelagic states with very small populations and little technological means.

Archipelagic states may designate archipelagic sea lanes in which all ships enjoy the right of passage. This is similar to transit passage in international straits.

The most consequential innovation is the establishment of the Exclusive Economic Zone in Part V of the Convention. The EEZ extends to a limit of 200 miles from the baselines, making it the most extensive territorial sea claim to date. Most of the states that had claimed a 200-mile territorial sea were able to adjust to the new concept and to sign the Convention. However, some of the hard-liners among the territorialists—Peru and Ecuador—were unwilling. Specification of territorial seas of 200 miles was inscribed in their constitutions, and although, in practical terms, the Exclusive Economic Zone would have adequately satisfied their needs, ideological and political reasons, nationalist pride, and reluctance to give up anything have prevailed—for the time being.

The territorial sea concept, as its very name implies, is a territorial concept. It bestows sovereignty over the twelve-mile ocean expanse, in the same sense in which a state enjoys sovereignty over its land territory. The EEZ concept is a functional concept. It does not bestow sovereignty over an area. It does bestow sovereign rights over the economic uses of an area, compatible with concurrent rights of other parties with regard to noneconomic uses of the same area. Thus it constitutes, in a way, the least malignant form of national aggrandizement.

Since it is the right to utilize and the duty to manage—not ownership—that the Convention bestows in the Exclusive Economic Zone, the EEZ concept is a perfect complement to the common heritage concept. As the two concepts continue to evolve, they are converging into one dynamic nonownership system in which management is delegated, in the one case, to an international organization which obviously consists, above all, of states, and in the other case, to a coastal state, which must necessarily cooperate closely with other states and international organizations and keep in mind the interests of mankind as a whole, present and future generations, through some degree of profit-sharing and through measures that will insure conservation of the environment and safety at sea.

The immediate drawbacks of Part V of the Convention, which defines the limits and the content of national jurisdiction, are well known, and they can be summarized as follows.

First, geographical happenstance, which attributes to some states extraordinarily wide expansions of ocean space and resources, to most states very little, and to some states less than nothing, will contribute in the immediate future to increased inequality among nations.

Second, the hope that the mere acquisition of ocean space and resources could alleviate the poverty of developing coastal states has been disappointed. After a decade of experience with the EEZ, the net result is that nothing has changed. Wealth, in fact, is not created by resources. It is a product of resources, capital, technology, and skilled manpower. As long as the latter three factors are scarce, development is illusory. In a recent study, George Kent[17] of the University of Hawaii has shown how fish, following the pattern of other commodities in this period of the postcolonial extraction economy, tend to flow from less developed to more highly developed countries. He found that "this is indicated by the fact that most countries purchase their fish imports from countries which are poorer (in terms of gross national product per capita) than those to which they send their fish exports." Fish trade, like other trade, takes place primarily between developed countries; very little is held between developing countries. When it takes place between developed and developing countries, it flows in the direction of the already overfed developed countries, away from the protein-deficient poorer countries. The introduction of the economic zone has done nothing to change this pattern.

Third, extension of national jurisdictions is creating a great number of boundary conflicts. In the Caribbean alone there exist as many as 105 actual or potential conflicts, perhaps creating a lawyer's paradise. It obviously constitutes an enormous waste of time, energy, and money which could be spent more constructively.

Fourth, if it was the intention of the Conference to define boundaries clearly, unambiguously, and in such a way as to forestall subsequent unilateral claims to further expansions of national jurisdiction, this hope is bound to be frustrated. There are sufficient loopholes in the definitions to make further claims possible. These loopholes are found

78

in the articles defining the baselines from which national ocean space is measured, the characteristics of islands entitled to an economic zone and a continental shelf, and the limits of the outer continental margin (see comments on Part VI).

Fifth, economic zones—even the largest ones—do not constitute "closed systems" and, therefore, self-sufficient units of management. If the burdens and responsibilities of management must be shared, so must benefits. This principle is not adequately developed in the Convention.

Finally, the control of a large economic zone by a small island, which in terms of population, manpower, and economic power is a "micro state," may cause considerable problems and invite new forms of colonialism and imperialism.

All these criticisms undoubtedly have their share of truth, and, like everything new, the economic zone concept will cause problems and displacements. However, these problems can be overcome by regional cooperation and integration, which will downgrade the importance of political boundaries; by strengthening the international organizations called upon to help coastal states solve their problems; and, proportional to this necessary assistance, by a degree of revenue-sharing, most likely in the form of an ocean development tax.

In the medium and long term, the concept of the EEZ is a constructive and productive one for a number of reasons. First, it transcends the traditional notion of territorial sovereignty and ownership. Second, it reconciles the interests of coastal states, maritime states, and, to some extent (which will have to be further elaborated on a regional basis), those between coastal and landlocked states. Third, it provides an institutional framework for a system of management. Finally, it provides an enormous incentive to developing coastal and island states to develop the scientific, technological, and manpower capacity as well as the legal and institutional infrastructure necessary to take advantage of the new potential. And it provides an equally strong incentive to undertake regional and international cooperation and integration.

Part VI of the Convention deals with the continental shelf. Not one of the most creative parts of the Convention, this part does represent a curious twisting of history and of reason. However, it also probably represents an inevitable compromise, not so much with the few "broad-margin" states or "margineers" (Canada, Argentina, India, Australia, among others) as with international oil power. Since the 1960s, the U.S.-based multinational oil companies have been pressing hard for the widest possible extension of national jurisdiction on the continental shelf. In this way, they can insure that not one drop of oil escapes to fall under international jurisdiction, with which they appear unwilling to come to terms.

This is a curious evolution of thought. The same oil companies resisted, with the same doggedness, the internal U.S. development which culminated in the Truman Declaration of 1945. This declaration brought the outer continental shelf, beyond a three-mile limit, from state jurisdiction to federal jurisdiction. The oil companies had fared well under the accustomed jurisdiction of Louisiana, Texas, and California. Dealing with the more powerful federal government presented unknowns. Some oil executives called it "creeping communism" and "the end of the oil industry as we know it." But it was not. The oil companies did well under federal jurisdiction, and once this was accepted as the new rule of the game, they wished to keep it that way and extend the jurisdiction as far as possible.

The federal government's takeover of jurisdiction from the state governments was based on the idea that the continental shelf was the natural prolongation of the continental land mass (hence the name, continental shelf). Thus it was to be subject to federal (continental) jurisdiction, so that benefits could be shared among all American states, whether they happened to be coastal or internal (landlocked). This was the argument of the advocates of the Truman Doctrine.

By 1958, when the Truman Doctrine was incorporated in the Geneva Convention on the continental shelf (UNCLOS I), the doctrine had been stood on its head. The continental shelf was no longer the "natural prolongation of the continental land mass"—which, in a way, could be defended from a scientific point of view. It had become the natural prolongation of the coastal state, which clearly had no basis in geology. The landlocked states, though undeniably part of the continental land mass, were left, literally, high and dry.

The pseudoscientific definition of the 1958 Convention quickly broke down in practice. The term "adjacent to the coast" was ill defined, and it became clear that the exploitability clause, extending jurisdiction as far as technology will permit exploitation of the shelf, made the shelf practically open-ended. The coastal states could divide not only enclosed or semienclosed seas, but the open oceans as well.

Part VI of the new Convention was intended to close this loophole, provide clearly defined limits, and halt further arbitrary, unilateral claims.

Did the 1982 Convention succeed any better than the 1958 Geneva Convention?

In the final analysis, the answer must be negative. The new definition has dropped the exploitability clause ("cars on this highway are subject to a speed limit of 50 miles per hour, except for those cars able to go faster"), and is based on a combination of three criteria: distance, depth, and thickness of terrigenous sediments (which grow thinner with the distance from the coast). Thus the limit of this "submerged prolongation of the land mass of the coastal State"—where it exceeds the 200-mile limit of the economic zone—is defined either (1) by a line connecting points (not more than sixty miles apart) at which the thickness of the sediment is not less than 1 percent of the shortest distance of that point from the foot of the slope, or (2) by a line connecting points not more than sixty miles from the foot of the slope. This, in turn, is defined (in the absence of evidence to the contrary) as the "point of maximum change in the gradient at its base."

This limit thus defined may not, furthermore, exceed a distance of 350 miles from the baselines from which the territorial sea is measured or a hundred nautical miles from the 2,500-meter isobath, that is, a line connecting points (presumably not more than sixty miles apart) where the superjacent water reaches a depth of 2,500 meters.

Future generations may look upon this definition as bizzarely Byzantine, likely to hide more than it reveals. The only thing that it safely insures is that oil stays under national jurisdiction. Where the sediments are less than one kilometer thick (or 1 percent of the distance of 100 kilometers from the foot of the slope), no oil is going to be found—at least not as far as oil geologists know today. This perspective may be upset, however, by future theories and discoveries.

The 350-mile overall limit (first proposed by the Soviet Union) is undoubtedly an improvement over the total open-endedness of the 1958 Convention, but it is as elastic as the baseline from which it is measured.

Exact identification of the foot of the slope and reliable measurement of the thickness of the sediments are formidable tasks, likely to leave, in most cases, a margin of doubt and uncertainty. These tasks would, furthermore, consume huge amounts of time and money, all for a purpose that is really not productive, or which undoubtedly produces deducted value.

The Convention establishes a laborious international commission to assist coastal states in the fulfillment of these tasks, for which they are given ten years after the Convention comes into force. During that time the International Sea-Bed Authority could be severely hampered in doing its job, considering the absence of clearly defined boundaries. This also includes the boundary of the continental shelf of Antarctica, about which the Convention says nothing.

Undoubtedly, future negotiations on the question are inevitable.

Would it not have been easier, and more logical, to follow the advice of the many landlocked and geographically disadvantaged states at the Conference—for example, the Arab states, many African states, Malta—and drop the whole pseudoscientific notion of a continental shelf as the natural prolongation of a coastal state, as well as the whole geopolitical romanticism of political boundaries defined by geological circumstances? This would require recognition that the continental shelf theory had been superseded by the economic zone theory, which gives the coastal state all economic rights on the seabed out to a 200-mile limit.

Would it not also have been easier to stipulate that oil, in all cases, goes under national jurisdiction, and to obtain in return the agreement that the mining of deep-sea hard minerals, in all cases, goes under the jurisdiction of the International Sea-Bed Authority, that is, go "functional" all the way?

One does not know. The fact is that when the Convention was drafted, it was not possible. Article 76, hotly debated over many years, was the best one could get. It was not the case of choosing between this convention or a better one. The choice was between this convention or none.

Part VI is not, however, without a silver lining. In one respect, in fact, it constitutes a breakthrough, and it sets a precedent which may be enormously important for the future. Article 82 establishes that the coastal states will make payments or contributions in kind with respect to exploitation of the nonliving resources of the continental shelf beyond 200 miles of the baselines from which the breadth of the territorial sea is measured, that is, beyond the limits of the economic zone. Payments and contributions are to be made annually with respect to all production at a site after the first five years of production. Thus a tax holiday is provided to enable the coastal state to recover its investment. From the sixth year on, the rate of payment or contribution is 1 percent of the value or volume of production at the site. The rate will increase by 1 percent for each subsequent year until the twelfth year, and will remain at 7 percent thereafter.

This is a seminal concept that may bring a sizable income to the International Sea-Bed Authority for development purposes from the exploitation of oil and gas—for example, off the coast of Newfoundland in Canada and in other places—as well as from the mining of polymetallic sulphides or cobalt crusts off the coasts of the Galapagos Islands, Oregon, Washington, and British Columbia or a number of U.S. island possessions in the Pacific. Even more important than the quantitative aspect is the qualitative aspect of this provision. Since, under the Convention, the coastal state enjoys exactly the same sovereign rights over all economic uses of the continental shelf beyond 200 miles as it does of the EEZ (there is a slight difference with regard to scientific research carried out by other states), it follows that, if a tax is "legal" on the shelf beyond 200 miles, it may well become equally "legal" for the EEZ (as it is already "legal" for land-based producers assisted by the revolving fund).

Thus in Part VI there has also been give and take: conciliation among almost irreconcilable clashes of interests, the resistance and inertia of the old, and the breakthrough of the new. Obviously such a dynamic process cannot generate perfection. It is not to be wondered, therefore, why the Convention is not better than it is. It is to be marvelled that it is as good as it is. Indeed, it is unique that such a degree of revolutionary innovation has been accepted peacefully through an orderly political process by such an overwhelming majority of the international community in the relatively short span of a decade and a half.

Part VII of the Convention, dealing with the high seas, is in many respects a relic from the past. It is an attempt to save what can be saved of the old principle of the freedom of the high seas (defined in Article 87). In many respects, this part harks back to the 1958 Convention on the high seas, covering such matters as the duty to render assistance to vessels in distress, prohibition of the transport of slaves, the duty to cooperate in the repression of piracy, illicit traffic in narcotic drugs or psychotrophic substances, and unauthorized broadcasting. Romantic or nostalgic as it may be, there are, however, hints in this part as well of a future common heritage regime for this vestige of the past, the high seas. Article 89 establishes that no state may validly purport to subject any part of the high seas to its sovereignty. This is in accordance with tradition and is considerably weaker than corresponding Article 137 on the international seabed, which is the common heritage of mankind: "No State shall claim or exercise sovereignty or sovereign rights over any part of the Area or its resources, nor shall any State or natural or judicial person appropriate any part thereof. No such claim or exercise of sovereignty or sovereign rights nor such appropriation shall be recognized." Basically the two articles mean the same thing.

Article 88 brings, perhaps, the most startling deviation from the 1958 Convention, for it establishes that "the high seas shall be reserved for peaceful purposes." This, again, would appear to bring the high seas one step closer to a common heritage system. The interpretation and development of this article will be one of the tasks of the forthcoming phase of establishing the new order in the oceans.

Finally, Section 2 of Part VII creates at least a rudimentary framework for the management and conservation of the living resources of the high seas, and refers its further development to cooperation between states and existing, or yet to be created, subregional and regional fisheries organizations. The faithful implementation of these articles, establishing an effective system of management for the living resources in the high seas, to complement and interact with the management systems created for the EEZ, will complete the process of bringing the high seas under a common heritage regime. This task is still ahead of us, but it is clearly anticipated in this document of transition.

Parts VIII and IX, dealing with the regime of islands and enclosed or semienclosed seas, respectively, are all too succinct and call for interpretation and development during the next phase.

Clearly, the definition of what is an island, in Article 121, is inadequate and bound to invite abuse and conflict. Paragraph 1 defines an island as "a naturally formed area of land, surrounded by water, which is above water at high tide." Paragraph 2 bestows on any such island the right to a territorial sea of twelve miles, a contiguous zone of another twelve miles, an economic zone of 200 miles, and a continental shelf as defined in Article 76. The exception, defined in paragraph 3, is an island that is, in fact, nothing but a rock that "cannot sustain human habitation or economic life of its own." Such islands shall have no EEZ or continental shelf.

These qualifications are remarkably imprecise. There is no hard and fast line between what can and what cannot sustain human habitation—and which country, let alone rock, can sustain today an economic life of its own? One can envision satellites spying in ocean areas characterized by volcanic activity to spot the sudden emergence from the waters of tiny islands (for example, Surtsey, near Iceland). This might then be followed by an island's swift occupation by a maritime power, the hasty establishment of human habitat (which can be sustained on the moon, or at the poles, or on the bottom of the sea), and the creation of some semblance of "economic life"—for example, an OTEC plant associated with some aquaculture. Then, lo and behold, a million square miles of economic zone may fall to the lot of these happy (or unhappy) occupants! To make this worst-case hypothesis even worse, it is—or may be in the near future—quite possible to act on nature and provoke the emergence of such islands by, for example, stimulating and directing volcanic activity. One could then expand one's empire over the seas.

In this context, the distinction between "naturally formed" and "artificial" islands breaks down, and there is no longer any reason why the one should be entitled to an EEZ and the other should not. The question of the attribution of a continental shelf is already complicated by the existence of atolls among the islands.

Needless to say, this is intellectual gamesmanship. It is serious enough, however, to indicate that the all too succinct Part VIII of the Convention needs interpretation and development.

Further development of Part IX of the Convention, dealing with enclosed or semienclosed seas, is already under way. This is, again, one of the amazing features of this Convention; it triggered broad trends and developments even before it was signed, and even before it was completed. This is one aspect that makes the work of UNCLOS III irreversible.

Part IX encourages states bordering enclosed or semienclosed seas to cooperate, among themselves or through appropriate regional or global organizations (existing or to be created), on matters pertaining to the management of living resources, the protection and conservation of the environment, and scientific research. Nonliving resources are not mentioned.

This part should be read in conjunction with articles in other parts of the Convention dealing with the management of living resources in the EEZ or on the high seas (Parts V and VII), with the protection of the environment (Part XII), and with the conduct of marine scientific research (Part XIII). These parts extend the same recommendations applied to enclosed or semienclosed seas, where the need is most obvious, to other coastal states bordering open oceans but sharing common interests and problems in ocean management.

The Regional Seas Programme was established in 1974 by the U.N. Environment Programme to implement the principles adopted by the Stockholm Conference on the Human Environment of 1972. Elaboration of a universal code of conduct for the protection of the environment, and the exhortation to cooperate on a regional basis, gave new impetus to this program. Between 1974 and 1984, it expanded with incredible vigor, and it now almost covers the world ocean with a network of regional cooperation and organization that involves over 110 coastal states, more or less the whole ocean-oriented sector of the U.N. family of organizations—FAO, IOC/UNESCO, IMO, UNCTAD, UNDP, and ILO (International Labour Organization)—and a great number of other intergovernmental and nongovernmental organizations. This upsurge of globe-spanning networks of regional cooperation and organization is unprecedented.

It would be premature to predict how successful this movement will be in the end. In the face of a protracted recession and some internal reorganization within UNEP, there are indeed signs that the movement may slacken and recede. Were this to happen, it would be a tremendous loss for the new international economic order, of which self-reliant regional cooperation is a cornerstone.

Regional organization plays three major roles in the new ocean regime.

Pertaining to the first role, universal norms must be articulated in terms adapted and applicable to local circumstances and further developed in accordance with local needs. Regional organization and regulation can thus function as a necessary link between universal rules and national law. In matters relating to the conservation of the marine environment, the United Nations Convention on the Law of the Sea provides a broad, comprehensive framework. It does not, however, provide an institutional infrastructure to translate universal principles into working reality. This task is left to the "competent international organizations."

The UNEP-initiated Regional Seas Programme is beginning to fill this gap and to provide the needed infrastructure.

The converging impulse from the national level, as already indicated in these pages, is the inextricable linkage between economics and ecology in the management of the EEZ. It transcends national zones even while creating them and, in turn, fosters an irresistible and unprecedented impulse toward regional cooperation and development.

Regional organization thus plays a second, enormously important two-way role: decentralizing from a universal level and centralizing, or integrating, from a national level. It is the first time in history that the globe is actually covered by a network of regional organizations, and these regions are primarily ecological and ocean-centered. This is a development whose importance cannot be overrated.

Regional organization may also be called upon to play a third important role in the establishment of an institutional infrastructure for the new "political ecosystem." This role may be one of providing a workable principle of representation.

As is well known, the so-called regional groups (African, Asian, Eastern European Socialist, Latin American, Western European and Others), though not constituted by any official document or rule of procedure, play an important role in the processes leading to decision making in the U.N. system, including UNCLOS III. In the Preparatory Commission for the International Sea-Bed Authority and for the International Tribunal for the Law of the Sea, the principle of decision making based on regional groups has been carried to a perfection of symmetry. The Commission's four special commissions and plenary are each entrusted with one of the five major tasks of the Commission. Each body is under the chairmanship of one of the five regional groups, and each body has four vice-chairmen representing the other four regional groups!

The only problem is that these five regional groups do not represent regions in any sense of the word. None of them comprises a membership with any degree of communality of interests and aspirations. Thus if instead of five regional groups one used the ten or twelve regional seas programs spanning the globe as a basis of representation and in the processes leading to decision making, an important step would be taken toward creating a political ecosystem that operates through new forms of decision making based on a synthesis of state, functional, and regional representation.

Part X, which defines the rights of access of landlocked states to and from the sea and freedom of transit, concludes the section of the Convention dealing with traditional law. It does not add much to the rights of landlocked states already existing under the 1965 Convention on transit of landlocked states. Not much, in fact, could be obtained for the landlocked states with regard to transit rights or to access to fisheries in the EEZ in a general, global framework where the role of one side consists of asking and the role of the other of giving. Regional cooperation and organization will provide a more suitable framework for the transformation of the role of the landlocked states in the context of technical advances in transportation (multimodal system), aquaculture, and the new attention being paid to the management of international rivers and waterways. Within this framework both landlocked and coastal states will have to give and take as equal partners in the sharing of common resources.

This summary of the traditional or systems-maintaining first section of the Convention has turned out longer than intended, for even this section contains a great deal that is startlingly new. Some of its articles are fraught with the danger of abuse and consequences perhaps not duly foreseen by UNCLOS III, while other articles open up new vistas of international cooperation and development. The negative aspects, however, would have existed even without the adoption of the Convention, and in that case, they would remain unmitigated in a world that, during the second half of the twentieth century, was heading straight for a carving up of the oceans, entailing inequity, conflict, pollution, and exhaustion of living resources. In contrast, the positive aspects would not have existed without the Convention, which clearly offers a new platform from which to strike out in new directions.

FIVE

A Constitution for the Oceans:

Systems-Transforming

With Parts XI–XV, we have reached the truly systems-transforming section of the Convention. Here UNCLOS III has created a new type of international organization, the International Sea-Bed Authority, based on the principle of the common heritage of mankind (Part XI). It has also articulated the first comprehensive framework for international environmental law (Part XII), an international regime for the conduct of marine scientific research (Part XIII), and the transfer of technology (Part XIV). Finally, it has established the first comprehensive system of binding dispute settlement in the history of international relations.

It could not have been expected that the International Sea-Bed Authority would have emerged perfect, like Botticelli's Venus, from the waves of the Conference. It turned out more like the first bicycle—quaint, in many ways ineffective or dysfunctional, and in need of long-term streamlining through practical experience. Nothing is born perfect, and the task of creating an institutional framework, a machinery to embody the new, and as yet little understood, principle of the common heritage of mankind, was staggeringly complex.

The clash of interests between North and South was violent. For example, the North wanted a weak interpretation of the principle of common heritage. It accepted

93

some degree of revenue-sharing through payments to the Authority, but, for the rest, wished to leave states and companies free to do business as usual. The South insisted on a strong interpretation of the principle, including not only revenue-sharing but also sharing of management prerogatives as well as technology transfer. The North wanted a weak Sea-Bed Authority, no more than an office for the registry of claims. The South wanted an Authority with comprehensive powers and responsibilities for management of the common heritage, which was to be entrusted to the Enterprise, the operational arm of the Authority—a first embodiment of the new international economic order. The North wanted cheaper resources and supplies independent of the control of "politically unstable" producer countries. The South wanted to secure the stability of commodity prices and the expansion of its land-based production. The North wanted to maximize private profit and minimize international contributions. The South wanted to maximize international contributions for the benefit of developing countries. The North was out to defend its technological advantage, while the South pressed for mandatory technology transfer, without which the common heritage of mankind might have remained nothing but a dream. The North wanted decision-making power in the governing bodies of the Authority, proportionate to its economic and technological power. The South wanted international democracy, based on the sovereign equality of all states, whether rich or poor. Finally, the South wanted a simple framework for the Authority, which could respond flexibly to changing circumstances. The North insisted on spelling out every administrative and financial detail in advance to reduce the discretionary power of the Authority to a minimum. And all this was for an industry whose future was uncertain and depended upon technological and economic variables impossible to quantify.

As if this did not suffice, neither the North nor the South is monolithic, and there were divergencies and problems between East and West, within the West itself, and within the various interest groups of the developing nations. One can thus imagine the difficulties of the negotiations. One can also imagine that the result could not be perfect. It is, nevertheless, a unique achievement, and the future, which has already begun, will take care of adjusting and adapting it to changing realities.

Organization of the International Sea-Bed Authority

The basic structure of the International Sea-Bed Authority is logical. It consists of an Assembly of State Members and a Council. The Assembly, the supreme body of the organization, is charged with laying down broad policy guidelines, undertaking a number of electoral functions, and confirming the budget. As in most international organizations, every state has one vote.

The Council, the executive body of the organization, is responsible for establishing the specific policies to be pursued by the Authority on any question or matter within its competence. In particular, it prepares slates of candidates for the Assembly for election to various offices; it establishes subsidiary bodies, including the highly important Legal and Technical Commission and Economic Planning Commission; and, most important, it issues directives to its operational arm, the Enterprise, and approves work plans and contracts with companies and states. The Council also takes measures to protect land-based producers from the adverse economic effects of ocean mining. It recommends to the Assembly rules, regulations, and procedures for the equitable sharing of financial and other economic benefits derived from activities in the international seabed area, and from the payments and contributions received for production on the continental shelf beyond 200 miles from shore. The Convention lists a number of other responsibilities for this centrally important body.

The Council consists of thirty-six members. Their election is based on a most complex combination of criteria of regional and interest group representation to assure adequate representation of the minorities of industrialized states, socialist states, and land-based producers, and to prevent any single interest group from blocking or imposing decisions.

The decision-making process is as complex as the composition of the Council. It consists of the so-called "three-tier" system (introduced by the United States), where some decisions require a two-thirds majority of votes, some more controversial decisions require a three-fourths majority, and the most sensitive and controversial decisions require a consensus. The latter concern, in particular, rules, regulations, and procedures; financial questions; and amendments.

The composition and decision-making process of the Council are undoubtedly cumbersome, reflecting the long and difficult process of negotiations which produced them. They raise a number of practical and theoretical questions.

From a practical point of view, it is difficult to imagine that a mining business could be run effectively this way, and in competition with private business operating in areas under national jurisdiction. From a theoretical point of view, it is questionable whether the introduction of interest representation is the best way to serve the real interests of a progressive international community. It might have been better to confine interest representation to the Enterprise, which should be a business, based on sound financial criteria. The Council, in contrast, should be a political body, based on democratic and permanent principles. Interest groups tend to shift over time. To freeze them in a constitution may cause long-term problems. Straight regional representation (the criterion underlying the composition of the General Committee of the Preparatory Commission) would have been far more appropriate.

Clearly the International Sea-Bed Authority integrates politics, economics, and science in a new way, and on this point, the Convention has broken new ground. In this sense, the Sea-Bed Authority will become a constitutional model for the future. It is inevitable, however, that the mechanism of this integration is not yet perfect. It will go through a period of practical experimentation, and may be adjusted at the Review Conference, which, in accordance with the Convention, is to take place fifteen years after commercial production commences in the international area.

The other principal organs of the International Sea-Bed Authority are the Secretariat, about which not much need be said as it follows the standard pattern of secretariats of international organizations, and the Enterprise, which is the operational arm through which the Authority can engage in seabed mining on its own.

The operational options of the Authority are, in fact, three. It can operate either through its own Enterprise, a public international corporative entity, provided it can muster the capital and the technology to compete effectively with the private sector, or through a licensing system under which states and companies obtain "contracts" to work on their own, subject to the control of the Authority. These two modes of operation constitute the so-called "parallel system" first proposed by U.S. Secretary of State Henry Kissinger. The third option, provided for and encouraged by the Convention, is joint ventures between the Enterprise and states or companies.

The parallel system is based on competition between the Authority and established industry, which is unfortunate. It raises insurmountable problems of capitalization and technology transfer, and it is the most cost-ineffective system that could have been devised. In the situation as it has developed since the drafting of the Convention, the industrialized states and their industries have the option to operate either under the jurisdiction of the Authority or in areas under national jurisdiction. Furthermore, production will not be restricted to manganese nodules but will include other resources, the management of which is not specified in the Convention. Thus it is easy to predict that the parallel system, in the sense provided for in the Convention, will not become fully operational. Attention will therefore focus on the third option—joint ventures or joint enterprises—where the Convention leaves a great deal of desirable flexibility and room for experimentation and which, with slight adaptations, could be operable in areas of national as well as international jurisdiction, provided that it offers tangible benefits to all parties concerned.

As is well known, the United States failed to sign the Convention because of its objections to the International Sea-Bed Authority as defined in Part XI of the Convention and its annexes. Obviously there are problems with Part XI—some of the major ones (overloading with detail, the inoperable parallel system, the inefficient decision-making process) are contributions of the U.S. delegation—but the technical objections put forward by the United States as a pretext for not signing are all flimsy and untenable and they can be, and have been, refuted one by one. It appears that the real objection of the United States was political and ideological. The whole idea of the common heritage of mankind and of a new type of relationship with developing countries is obviously opprobrious to the Reagan Administration.

The U.S. counterproposal, the so-called Mini Treaty or Reciprocating States Agreement or Interim Agreement, was so controversial politically and legally that it never had any chance. At present, all ocean-mining states, with the exception of the United States, the United Kingdom, and the Federal Republic of Germany, have signed the Convention. The U.K. and Germany are members, however, of the European Economic Community (EEC), which has signed the Convention and is a member of the Sea-Bed Authority. Since these two countries, within the EEC Council, did not object to this decision, it is rather unimportant whether they, individually, have signed the Convention or not. They are covered by it through the EEC. This then definitely eliminates any prospect of an alternative Mini Treaty regime as attempted by the United States, except in the most unlikely case that the Convention fails to come into force. If, in the future, the United States insists on mining outside the Convention regime, it will do so in areas under national jurisdiction, through bilateral agreements with coastal states.

The International Sea-Bed Authority—its origin, its evolution through the dialectics of interests and negotiations, and its value as a model for the future—is unique in the history of international relations and in the history of institution building. Its value for the future is that it confronts, for the first time, the issues described briefly below. Whether establishment of the Authority solved these issues totally or only partly is unimportant. What is important is that it did so practically by a consensus of the entire international community—East, West, North, and South.

First, operative public or private international institutions have existed before, of which Intelsat, and particularly Inmarsat, are prime examples. The Sea-Bed Authority, however, with its Enterprise system which is not only operative but also productive in the primary sector with the potential of generating an income of its own, carries the concept considerably further. Public/private international institutions may play an increasingly important role in world economics.

Second, the Sea-Bed Authority has the power to impose an international tax. In a number of sectors, international taxes must be an essential part of a new international economic order.

Third, the Sea-Bed Authority, for the first time, brings multinational companies under control through a structured relationship, and does it far more effectively than a mere code of conduct could ever hope to do.

Fourth, the Sea-Bed Authority attempts a new form of integration of politics, economics, and science.

Fifth, the Sea-Bed Authority represents an attempt at global production planning. This is needed as well for other sectors of the economy if large-scale starvation and increasing imbalances are to be avoided.

Sixth, the Sea-Bed Authority integrates environmental considerations in its production policy.

Seventh, although the Sea-Bed Authority does not mandate technology transfer, which, at this stage, would be unacceptable not only to the free-enterprise countries but equally to the socialist industrialized countries, it certainly encourages and facilitates technology transfer and establishes mechanisms for settling disputes that may arise from technology transfer. It also offers developing countries a unique opportunity for acquiring skills in managing high-technology enterprises.

Eighth, the Sea-Bed Authority is endowed with the technological and institutional mechanisms for surveillance and verification in the deep seabed. Although legally this capacity is restricted to verification of compliance with the rules and regulations relating to mining activities, it could well be expanded at a later stage to verification of compliance with the terms of the Treaty on the Prohibition of the Emplacement of Nuclear Weapons and Other Weapons of Mass Destruction on the Sea-Bed and the Ocean Floor and in the Subsoil Thereof, adopted by the United Nations in 1971. The requisite technologies are identical. Thus the Authority might make a significant contribution in the sphere of disarmament and arms control, where the verification issue is a crucial component.

Finally, the Sea-Bed Authority is based on, and provides an institutional framework for, the principle of the common heritage of mankind, which must become the fundamental principle of a new international economic order.

International Law

Parts XII–XIV of the Convention also break new ground in international law.

Marine Environment

Part XII deals comprehensively with all sources of pollution in the marine environment, whether ship-borne, generated by seabed mining, carried through the atmosphere, or land-based. On the question of enforcement, the Convention comes up with a most original solution, balancing the interests of coastal states with those of maritime shipping states.

Coastal states, evidently, have a keen interest in protecting their shores against ship-borne pollution, and they want national rights to do so. The shipping nations, naturally, fear that these rights may encroach on their freedom of navigation. Presumably, freedom of navigation includes some degree of freedom to pollute. Port states share the interests of both coastal and shipping nations. Ports, obviously, are part of coastal states, but, at the same time, their livelihood depends on shipping and a flourishing seaborne trade.

Thus the Convention bestows the greatest enforcement power on port states. According to the Convention, once a ship has put into a port, the port state may initiate procedures against a polluter no matter where the pollution took place—under the port state's jurisdiction, under the jurisdiction of another state, or on the high seas.

As far as the effective protection of the marine environment is concerned, the problem remains that port states may take action, but it is not an obligation—an obligation that might have been too burdensome. Here then is a task for environmentalists in the coming decade: raise the consciousness in port states; generate a new sense of responsibility in their citizens and governments; and create, as it were, a new worldwide Hanseatic League of Port States, which would act through the Regional Seas Programme for the protection of the marine environment and the enforcement of rules and standards laid down in the framework of Part XII of the Convention.

On March 2, 1983, Iraqi bombers hit an already leaking Iranian oil installation in the Nowruz offshore oil field, about sixty kilometers from the Kharg Island oil port. They also hit six other wells nearby. Infernal flames lit the sky by night and black smoke covered the sun by day. Week after week passed. When the flames died down, the oil continued to pour forth into the Persian Gulf, at a rate of about ten thousand barrels a day. As the oil slick grew to about twelve thousand square miles in size, the winds carried it southward and spread it until it threatened the entire semienclosed Gulf and the coasts of Saudi Arabia and Qatar, reaching for the Straits of Hormuz and the Indian Ocean. Fish and fowl were dying everywhere, dead turtles and dolphins were stranded. The mighty bodies of more than fifty dugongs—almost the entire known Gulf population of this endangered species—were found floating in the oil or washed ashore. Ports closed down, and a foul odor rose over the Gulf. The international community looked on aghast at this unprecedented disaster, involving warring and nonwarring states alike and destroying the sea and its living and nonliving resources.

On March 29, the nineteen oil companies operating in the Gulf issued a statement warning that the unchecked leakage would turn the Gulf into one vast oil lake, and that it had the potential for unprecedented environmental and ecological damage. By May, the giant oil slick had reached the coasts of Bahrain and Qatar.

Some observers hoped that the leak would force an end to the two-year-old war that was lacerating the region and threatening world peace. The parties would have no choice but to get together to repair the damage. The Regional Organisation for the Protection of the Marine Enrivonment called a meeting for April 3–7. However, neither Iran nor Iraq attended, and the meeting failed to produce any results, as did a subsequent meeting of Gulf States foreign ministers on April 16.

In October 1983, Iran succeeded in capping one of the runaway wells, although it is not known whether this operation was 100 percent successful. In any case, at this writing the oil from the other wells continues to flow.

It remains extremely difficult to assess the damage from this leakage because of the many conflicting reports from inside and outside the region. It is now known, for instance, that many of these reports, including one using satellite images, were deliberately distorted by unscrupulous business interests. Another complicating factor was that polluters, using the Nowruz spill as cover, took the opportunity to dump wastes into the Gulf.

Whatever the precise dimensions of this disaster, oil pollution of the oceans increased globally by a factor of 930 percent during 1983, according to the British Oil Spill Intelligence Report.[18] And this was largely due to the ongoing situation in the Gulf.

Neither the United Nations Convention on the Law of the Sea nor the Regional Seas Programme, initiated in the 1970s by UNEP, with its conventions, protocols, and plans of action, has any consolation to offer in such a situation. They deal with pollution arising from peaceful uses of the seas, heedless of the fact that the worst of all polluters is war. Another fact, not often noted, is that in our age the boundaries between peace and war are becoming blurred as international and civil wars increasingly interact, with partisans, guerrillas, and terrorists taking up arms alongside and across the lines of regular armies, and the number of civilian casualties exceeding that of the military. With the progressive disintegration of the concept of national sovereignty has come the disintegration of the concept of international war—that is, wars that started at a precise date with a declaration of war, and ended at a precise date with the surrender of one party, followed by a peace treaty. There has also been a disintegration of the very concept

103

of "weapon." Modern weapons of mass destruction consist of technologies which, without much transformation, have peaceful as well as military applications (for example, atomic energy, chemical and biological agents, outer-space and deep-sea technologies, and lasers and electronics). At such a time, it may be futile to try to insist on a clear-cut distinction between peaceful uses and military uses, and to provide for the ones while trying to ignore the others. This is an aspect of the problem that still awaits attention and action.

Could one imagine a protocol or convention incorporated into the action plans of the Regional Seas Programme providing for relief of environmental disaster, not only in case of peace but also in case of war? The purpose of such a protocol or convention would be (1) to prohibit warlike measures or the use of weapons in relation to installations, oil wells, atomic energy plants, or other establishments similar in nature which cause or may cause extensive and irreversible damage to the environment; (2) to establish the obligation of warring states to prevent irreversible damage to the environment; and (3) to protect neutral states against damages arising from a war in which they have no part.

Such an instrument would be both preventive and remedial. The preventive part would consist of a reciprocal agreement among all participating states, declaring that installations whose destruction would cause irreversible damage to the environment or damage to third parties, such as oil wells or atomic energy plants, are immune and cannot be attacked in case of armed conflict or insurrection. The Hague conventions of 1907 contain similar exemptions (Article 24) for hospitals, churches, historical monuments, or open cities. Other conventions that confirm these principles, such as the Fourth Geneva Convention of 1949 or the 1975 Covenant on Human Rights in Armed Conflict, could be cited. Unfortunately, these rules have been swept away by the introduction of the modern weapons of mass destruction and the general disintegration of the concept of war. Perhaps the time has come to reconsider these rules in the new context, in this era beyond peace and war.

One also could invoke the Convention on the Prohibition of Military or Any Other Hostile Use of Environmental Modification Techniques. For whether such modification is intentional or a by-product of "conventional" destructive activities, it is still environmental modification. This opinion is shared by the editor of the above-cited British Oil Spill Intelligence Report, Richard Golob, who, in introducing the report, said: "That was one of the first times in history when the environment was used as a way to wage war."[18] Prohibiting attacks on oil wells and nuclear energy plants would thus be a way of implementing the convention forbidding environmental warfare.

Immunity against war damage of such installations would, of course, be a tremendous bonus, not only to neutral states and the environment, but also to warring states and especially to their industries. The question then arises as to whether there should be a *quid pro quo.* The protocol or convention might, in fact, have some features of an insurance contract, for which the insured parties pay a premium.

Precedents exist for this kind of agreement as well. The 1979 convention on oil pollution and the establishment of a special fund in the Gulf in 1978 come immediately to mind, but they apply to peacetime accidents. What is new in the present proposal is that it combines a principle familiar in the law of war with one relating to peaceful uses.

The premiums, which may be rather substantial considering the magnitude of the damage against which they insure, could be paid to a special fund, perhaps within UNDP, to be utilized for development purposes, including, above all, reconstruction in the war-ravaged region.

The remedial part of the protocol or convention should provide that, if damage occurs in spite of the immunity of the installations concerned, there must be an immediate cease-fire. The cease-fire should be wide enough and of sufficient duration to permit the establishment of a safety zone around the damaged installation and its repair by a crew of technicians from neutral states.

In March 1983, it would have taken two days to repair the damaged wells in the Gulf, according to U.S. experts. By July, it would have taken two months. Now, the damage is becoming irreversible. Such a situation might be prevented by the remedial part of the protocol if it were freely entered on a reciprocal basis by the states of a region in peacetime.

Aside from its environmental effect, which is of the utmost importance, such a protocol or convention would also have an arms control effect by establishing sanctuaries or weapon-free zones. Moreover, through the "insurance premiums" to be paid, it would have a development effect, as it would generate funds for development purposes. The use of such multipurpose agreements will become more widespread in the future. Considering the close interrelationship of issues, not only in the oceans, they offer the only hope for success.

Marine Scientific Research and Technology Transfer

Part XIII of the Convention provides a general framework for the conduct of scientific research under the new ocean regime. The fact that scientific research conducted in areas under the jurisdiction of coastal states now requires the consent of that state, as well as the fact that the area in which scientific research can be freely conducted has thus been considerably reduced, have given rise to concern in some quarters. Certainly this coastal state right—as any other right—may be abused or misused, entailing bureaucratic procrastination which may hamper research. Such delays and problems may not be beneficial to the coastal state, the researching state, or the international community as a whole. These concerns may, however, be more theoretical than practical.

Part XIII does introduce a number of highly positive aspects. For example, scientific research, which was previ-

106

ously slighted or ignored by the law of the sea, is given an enormously important place in the Convention. It is indeed extraordinary that, out of 320 articles, almost 100 or almost one-third deal in one way or another with marine scientific research.

Another positive aspect is that marine scientific research, for the first time in any legal instrument, is reserved exclusively for peaceful purposes. Clearly this applies only to the international protection and enhancement of scientific research. The Convention is, obviously, impotent with regard to military applications of marine scientific research within national jurisdiction. It is nevertheless significant as it moves scientific research toward the concept of the common heritage of mankind, of which it clearly is an important part.

In this regard, it is important to note that the Convention encourages, and even mandates, international cooperation in marine scientific research. A number of articles, in fact, begin by postulating, "States shall cooperate. . . ."

Finally, the Convention enhances the internationalization of marine scientific research—that is, the conduct of marine scientific research under international auspices. Article 247 provides that if a project to carry out research in an area under the jurisdiction of a coastal state has been approved by an international organization, further consent by the coastal state is not needed, provided only that the state is a member of such organization and did not object to the adoption of the project by that organization. This then enhances international planning of research, as well as international sponsorship, which guarantees that a project has no direct military or commercial implications.

Part XIII, as well as Part XIV which deals with technology transfer, encourages regional cooperation and mandates the establishment of regional centers of excellence for marine scientific research, training, and the transfer of technology. The Convention does not specify, however, how these centers should be financed. Once again, an ocean development tax seems the most practical solution to this problem.

Whereas Part XI creates a new institution for resource management and painstakingly prescribes its structure and functions, Parts XII–XIV do not create new infrastructure. They do, however, impose heavy new responsibilities on the existing international institutions presently engaged in marine scientific research, the protection of the environment, and the transfer of technology* and call for a strengthening and restructuring of these organizations.

The Executive Director's Special Report to UNIDO IV (1984) has already proposed the establishment of an international center for marine industrial technology, which might be instrumental in setting up the regional centers within the already existing framework of the Regional Seas Programme. The proposed center could also coordinate and integrate the policies of the regional centers to ensure that they serve the best interests of each region and of the international community as a whole.

In this context the Convention again appears as an instrument of transition. The next phase of ocean development will be as challenging as the one that culminated in the adoption of the Convention in 1982.

Binding Dispute Settlement System

Institution-building and systems-transforming, Part XV of the Convention establishes a comprehensive binding dispute settlement system. It is indeed the first time in the history of treaty-making that a global convention imposes that disputes between states' parties concerning the inter-

---

*These institutions include FAO, living resources; IOC/UNESCO, physical and chemical oceanography and marine geology; World Meteorological Organization (WMO), ocean-related meteorology; UNEP, the environment; UNIDO, technology transfer; UNCTAD, socioeconomic, ocean-related subjects; IMO, safety of navigation; and the Ocean Economics and Technology Branch (OETB), ocean mining.

pretation or application of the Convention must be submitted to arbitration or adjudication at the request of either party, with the award or decision being binding for the other party.

States have a wide range of options as to the method of dispute settlement, from conciliation to arbritration to adjudication by the International Court of Justice in The Hague, or by the newly established International Tribunal for the Law of the Sea in Hamburg, whose statute is set forth in an annex to the Convention.

Disputes concerning the interpretation or application of Part XI of the Convention (on seabed mining) go to a special Sea-Bed Chamber of the International Tribunal for the Law of the Sea. Before this chamber not only states have a standing but also "juridical persons," who may be companies, consortia, or even individuals. In this way, individuals become subject to international law. This represents a leap forward in the development of global international law, although it is already accepted at the regional level (European Human Rights Court).

Disputes concerning fisheries, scientific research, navigation, or the environment may go to special arbitration tribunals to be established by FAO, UNESCO, IMO, and UNEP, respectively. This implies another novel responsibility for these organizations. At the same time, Part XV also beautifully ties together all the disparate elements touched on by the Convention and thus provides the first piece of needed integrative machinery.

It is true that there are some loopholes in this system. Certain types of disputes on sensitive subjects, most liable to generate conflict, are exempted from compulsory settlement. These include disputes regarding boundary delimitation and military activities, and those over which the Security Council of the United Nations has jurisdiction. Activities in the economic zone are also not subject to compulsory settlement unless they concern the international rights of other states in the zone, such as navigation, overflight, or the laying of cables or pipelines. These exemptions are inevitable concessions to the system of sovereign states in which we live. They do not alter the fact that Part XV starts a new chapter in the history of international dispute settlement.

A first attempt—strangely forgotten during subsequent negotiations—to attach a binding dispute settlement system to a global treaty relating to the law of the sea was made by Brazil during the early days of negotiations on the 1971 Treaty on the Prohibition of the Emplacement of Nuclear Weapons and Other Weapons of Mass Destruction on the Sea-Bed and the Ocean Floor and in the Subsoil Thereof. Many delegates, at the time this treaty was negotiated, recognized and emphasized that any system of verification of compliance with the regulations of the treaty would be more acceptable if states members were assured of a fair settlement of disputes that might arise from verification procedures.

The next step should be to link these two instruments— the 1971 treaty dealing with the disarmament aspect (reservation for exclusively peaceful purposes) and the 1982 Convention dealing with the development aspect (peaceful uses) of the common heritage concept—and to give the new International Tribunal for the Law of the Sea, which did not exist when the 1971 treaty was adopted, jurisdiction over disputes arising from verification procedures under that treaty. This would require an amendment to the 1971 treaty during the next review conference. As far as the 1982 Convention is concerned, the powers of the International Tribunal for the Law of the Sea are already sufficiently comprehensive to include this additional responsibility. This would increase the efficacy of both instruments and the contribution of the Law of the Sea to the maintenance and enhancement of peace.

Organizing for the Future

The future is in our hands. The fact that the Convention is, in a way, unfinished business, an instrument of transition, entails as many dangers as it generates opportunities. If mankind is bent on a suicidal course, it will seek out the loopholes and ambiguities in the Convention. States will continue the escalation of national claims in the pursuit of short-range, real or unreal, perceived interests. And depletion of resources, pollution of the environment, and militarization of ocean space will proceed unchecked toward final catastrophe.

But things need not go that way. The international community, while partly or intermittently clinging to those wonted ways, may continue to build on the incredible and unique basis laid down by UNCLOS III and the Convention on the Law of the Sea. Thus the fact that the Convention is unfinished and open-ended is an advantage, leaving the next generation of international institution-builders the flexibility they need to adapt the evolving structure to their own circumstances and requirements.

Two interdependent stages of further development can be envisaged.

The first is implicit in the text of the Convention itself: the principle enshrined in the preamble which says that all problems of the oceans are closely interrelated and must be considered as a whole; in the new responsibilities imposed on the "competent international organizations"; and in the reservation of the seabed, the high seas, and marine scientific research for peaceful purposes.

If one wanted to translate these implications into a series of political actions, the following agenda would emerge. First, the "competent international organizations" dealing with ocean space and resources must be strengthened and restructured. They must also be made more operational and responsive to local and regional needs. This, in turn, requires a broader financial basis and a degree of automaticity of international revenues.

111

Second, fora must be created for formulating integrated ocean policy, transcending the sectoral approach characterizing ocean policymaking in the past, whether on the national or international level. This should be done by articulating a dialogue between national, regional, and functional (global) interests.

Third, "peaceful uses" (development) and "reservation exclusively for peaceful purposes" (disarmament) must be reintegrated as the two, inseparable facets of the common heritage concept.

Most coastal states have already initiated the process of bringing their national legislation into line with the new international Law of the Sea and of creating national infrastructure to implement ocean policy under the new ocean regime, especially management of the economic zone. A number of developing as well as developed countries have already established ministries for ocean development, national agencies for aquatic resource management, etc., integrating fragments from various government departments (external affairs, defense, agriculture and fisheries, mines and energy, ports and harbors, commerce, tourism, science and technology) which have been dealing with various aspects of the marine environment and resources (Figure 1).

At the other end of the spectrum, most of the global "competent international organizations" (Table 5) have already established regional offices in a number of the oceanic regions listed in Tables 6 and 7. This process should be continued until all the organizations have regional offices in all the regions.

A Scheme of Regional Cooperation and Organization

It has been stressed in these pages that regional cooperation and organization are important in articulating global norms and standards and adjusting them to local needs and in complementing and integrating local institutions

112

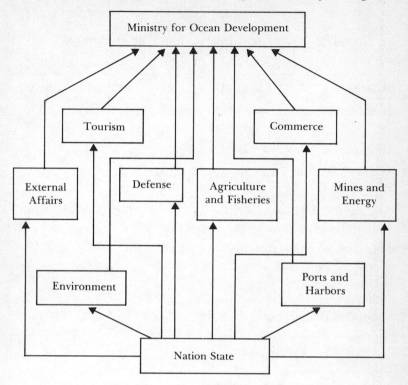

FIGURE I
National infrastructure

where management issues transcend the boundaries of national jurisdiction. The scheme proposed here illustrates how this could be achieved—utilizing only existing structures and ongoing processes—to realize a rational new economic order in the oceans. The purpose is certainly not to create costly new bureaucracies, whether national or international, but to rationalize existing ones and to establish linkages that would enable them to function more efficiently.

Each regional office should be headed by a regional secretary, appointed by the international organization from

TABLE 5
The "competent international organizations"

Activity	Organization in charge
Law of the Sea	U.N. Secretariat
Management of living resources	FAO/COFI
Management of nonliving resources	ISA
Management of the environment	UNEP, IMO, IAEA
Shipping and navigation	IMO, UNCTAD
Marine sciences	UNESCO, IOC
Marine technology	UNIDO, OETB
Coastal management	OETB
Marine labor	ILO
Marine health	WHO

COFI — Committee on Fisheries (FAO); ISA — International Sea-Bed Authority; IAEA — International Atomic Emergy Agency; WHO — World Health Organization.

a slate of candidates nominated by the states of the region. For example, IOC/UNESCO would have a regional secretary in the Mediterranean, the Caribbean, etc., nominated by the states of the region and appointed by IOC/UNESCO.

The regional secretaries in each region, together with one representative from each state of the region, would then form the Regional Commission for Ocean Development and Environment. The representatives of the states of the region would normally be the minister for ocean development or secretary-general of the national agency for aquatic resources. The Regional Commission would

TABLE 6
Action plans of the Regional Seas Programme

Action plan	Date
Mediterranean Action Plan and Barcelona Convention	1976
Kuwait Action Plan and Regional Convention	1978
Caribbean Action Plan (Regional Convention in preparation)	1981
West and Central African Action Plan and Regional Convention	1981
East African Action Plan (initiated)	
East Asian Action Plan	1981
Red Sea and Gulf of Aden Action Plan and Regional Convention	1982
South West Pacific Action Plan	1982
South East Pacific Action Plan Regional Convention	1981 1982
South West Atlantic Plan (initiated)	

TABLE 7
Other ocean regions

Baltic Sea	Arctic Basin	North Atlantic
North Sea	Southern Ocean	Black Sea

define an integrated ocean policy, approve a budget and raise the necessary funds, and elect a secretary-general. The Regional Commission would also establish special regional commissions for living and for nonliving resources,

115

environment, navigation, ports and harbors, water management, marine scientific research, training and transfer of marine technology (this commission would be responsible for establishing the regional center proposed by the Convention), and monitoring, surveillance, and multifunctional enforcement. There also should be a regional tribunal for the settlement of regional disputes, with the option of appeal to the International Tribunal for the Law of the Sea.

Such developments are not utopian; they have been fully initiated in various regions. An excellent example is the recent initiative of the Economic Commission for Latin America (ECLA). The Regional Programme of Action for Latin America, adopted by the Commission at Montevideo in 1981, contains a list of objectives which the Latin American countries have set for themselves to implement an international development strategy. Among these objectives are the following:

— Speed up economic and social development and the structural change of the national economies insofar as the use of ocean resources is concerned.

— Speed up development of the region's scientific and technological capacities for the use of its ocean spaces.

— Exhaust the means by which the products of the sea may help to combat hunger and malnutrition on the continent—as a way of eradicating poverty as rapidly as possible—and use suitable mechanisms for capturing, producing, consuming, and marketing these products within the region.

— Stimulate the economic, social, and political participation of those sectors which gain their livelihood by exploiting the sea.

— Conserve the quality and increase the potential use of the environment, including measures to correct wasteful practices and thereby improve living conditions and lay the

116

basis for a type of development which can be maintained in the long term.

— Define the potential for using the energy derived from the sea in the context of the development of new and renewable sources.

— Effectively exercise full sovereignty over the ocean resources and the common activities related to them.

— Strengthen integration of the different forms of cooperation among countries of the region to make better use of the ocean's resources, increase trade, and reinforce the capacity for joint negotiations in international fora so as to secure a more adequate position in the world economy.

— Promote changes in the structures of external economic relations relevant to the ocean dimension so as to achieve a new international economic order and the proposals of the Charter of Economic Rights and Duties of States.

The ECLA considers it essential that this program

design arrangements for inter-agency consultation in which the United Nations Secretariat, acting through its office and departments (Law of the Sea Affairs Section, Ocean Economics and Technology Branch, Department of Technical Cooperation for Development, Centre on Transnational Corporations), FAO, UNESCO, the Intergovernmental Oceanographic Commission (IOC), the Secretariat of the Conference on New and Renewable Energy Sources, etc., and ECLA itself, can formulate their points of view, suggestions and proposals for joint work and present their needs. This initial encounter could provide a foundation for permanent machinery for communication in the future and a support for those components of the United Nations system which are active in the region and have responsibility for marine affairs.[19]

Similar developments are under way in the Indian Ocean under the initiative of the Asian-African Legal Consulta-

117

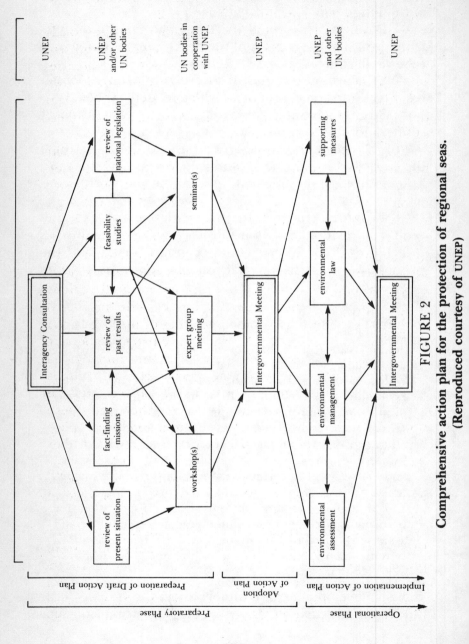

FIGURE 2

Comprehensive action plan for the protection of regional seas.
(Reproduced courtesy of UNEP)

tive Committee. UNEP's Regional Seas Programme works with the scheme reproduced in Figure 2.

A systematic effort must now be made to define exactly which countries are members of which region. At present there is still a tendency for each of the specialized agencies to go its own way and define its own region for its own function, thus creating an overlap between regions. A clear definition of the regions is essential for the establishment of efficient multifunctional management systems.

The next step is to articulate the interrelationship between the regional commissions and the global international organizations. One important link is already created by the proposed provision that the global organizations (FAO, UNEP, IOC, IMO, etc.) appoint secretaries in each region. In this regard, it is suggested that interregional councils be created, consisting of the regional secretaries in each category—for example, one interregional council would comprise FAO secretaries from all regions. These councils should be attached as second consultative chambers to the decision-making bodies of the U.N. agencies. Thus IOC, for example, would have two chambers: its executive council as it now exists and the interregional council of the secretaries of all special regional commissions for the management of marine science. Such an arrangement would considerably strengthen the operational capacity of the global organization and create a two-way linkage between global planning and regional operations.

Interdisciplinary, cross-sectoral planning of ocean policy is necessary, not only at the national and regional levels but at the global level as well. Hence a forum must be created to formulate such a policy. The most practical way to achieve this would be the establishment of a joint assembly of the general assemblies or policymaking bodies of the specialized agencies or "competent international organizations," coordinated by the Law of the Sea Secretariat of the United Nations. This joint assembly would meet every

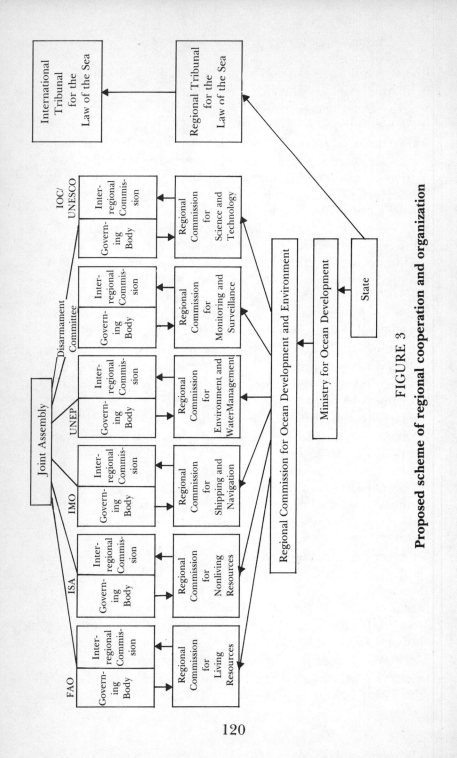

FIGURE 3

Proposed scheme of regional cooperation and organization

120

two years and would consider the problems of the oceans as a whole, with their inseparable linkages. No other forum would be able to undertake this task. Policy would thus have to be made jointly. The execution of policies would be left to each agency, which would retain its full autonomy and self-management.

This system would have the advantage of building on what has been already done. All the building blocks are, or are about to be, there: the mandate of the Convention; the departments for ocean development in different countries; the ecological/economic pressure for regional cooperation, if the new wealth of the oceans is to be realized at all; the regional programs; and the "competent international organizations." Thus the problem is one of architecture, not of building material, and what is needed is a design to integrate the material. The scheme proposed here and illustrated in Figure 3 may be feasible in this regard.

This scheme, which is flexible and open to further development, is a system of modules, some of which may be taken off when they are no longer functional, while others, responding to new needs or opportunities, may be added. The scheme is not a "supergovernment" touching on questions of sovereignty, but a functional federation of international organizations.

New International Order

At this point one can move on to a second stage, which transcends ocean space and resources. At this stage the new order for the oceans would become a model for, and part of, a new international order in general. That it should fulfill this role is inherent in the very nature of the uses of the oceans, which include the production of food and fiber, minerals and metals, energy, science and technology—in short, the whole range of human economic and cultural activities, all of which include, but transcend, the oceans.

121

Thus, given the overlap of problems and interests in the changing Antarctic regime and the ocean regime, one could consider adding an Antarctic module to the system. This would allow the Antarctic regime to retain its autonomy, while ensuring coordination and integration between Antarctic policy and ocean policy where needed (for example, in the management of living resources in the southern ocean, in the establishment of a mineral mining system in which all interested states might share, in the protection of the environment, in scientific research, and in the definition of boundaries).

The same also applies to outer space. The ocean regime utilizes satellites for resource exploration, meteorological research, and navigational aids. In fact, Inmarsat is an international organization that specializes in marine satellites. The outer-space and moon regime is a common heritage regime. Furthermore, deep-sea and outer-space technologies are closely interrelated and cooperation in scientific research and technology transfer would benefit both regimes. Thus the addition of an outer-space module that links the outer-space and moon regimes to the ocean regime would be logical.

Ocean energy will have to be integrated into general energy distribution grids and into regional and global energy planning. It is indeed bizarre that the United Nations has not yet established an energy organization. Energy is no less fundamentally important than food to the world economy. Moreover, food and energy problems interact. Thus since there is a Food and Agriculture Organization of the United Nations, there is no reason why there should not be an energy organization. It has, in fact, been proposed at various times, and sooner or later it must be established. When that time comes, an energy module might be added to the ocean system.

A multifunctional module for monitoring, surveillance, and enforcement might add the needed disarmament and arms control dimension to the system.

Then the time may have come for new, evolutionary developments in the United Nations system as a whole. All the building blocks would be there, and the design for a modular system of functional federations of international organizations, tied together by a policymaking General Assembly and a binding dispute settlement system, would, theoretically, not be too difficult, with the ocean system as a nucleus.

There is a long way to go toward establishment of such a system—having put into place thus far just one little submodule, the International Sea-Bed Authority, which still needs a lot of work. But for those who want to see, it opens new perspectives. The importance of the successful conclusion of the Third United Nations Conference on the Law of the Sea for the future of international organization and cooperation cannot be overrated.

SIX

The Philosophy of the Common Heritage

"Our whole attitude towards the oceans must change," said the President of Mexico Luis Echeverria, in addressing the first working session of the United Nations Conference on the Law of the Sea in 1974. A change in our attitude toward the oceans, however, implies a change in our attitude toward nature in general. And nature, of course, includes ourselves.

When we speak of a philosophy of the common heritage, we do not mean the concept of the common heritage. We are referring instead to the ideological and philosophical setting required for the application of that concept. The notions of peace and development and the protection of man and nature do not reside in a legal and institutional framework or in an economic theory, as necessary as these may be. In the final analysis, they reside in the minds of men.

The industrial revolution, as noted in Chapter 3, was and is inextricably rooted in Western philosophy and religion. It rests, ultimately, on the particular belief that man is the overlord of nature, and that nature is the servant of mankind. The divine right and God-given power to subject nature and to kill, maim, and exterminate nonhuman life are hardly conducive to a policy of conservation of nature.

It is true that Franciscan love for God's creatures derives from this Occidental tradition as well as the doctrines of the struggle for survival and human supremacy. But it was this latter doctrine, not Franciscan philosophy, that gave rise to modern civilization and the spirit of ruthless domination over nature.

It is also true that people closer to nature, having a philosophical tradition of continuity and contiguity with nature and professing nature-friendly philosophies, have trodden on one another ruthlessly in fanatic racial and religious altercations. They have done—and keep doing—this, however, not because of, but in spite of, their philosophy.

The fact is that we see the "outside" world with the same eyes as the "inside" world—that is, ourselves. On the one hand, pessimism about ourselves is inseparable from pessimism about the world in which we live. Cynicism and hatred are directed inward as much as outward. On the other hand, the commandment that we love our neighbor as much as ourselves is not so much a commandment as it is a statement of fact, for the continuity between "outside" and "inside" is much greater than the individualistic and, therefore, dualistic (I–other) philosophies of the West would have it.

Modern science is contributing to the blurring of the boundaries of the individual: in space, by the prospect, already partly realized, of organ transplants; in time, by disaggregating the concept of death (heart death; brain death; artificial life-support machines, with the precise moment of "death," which delimits individuality, becoming uncertain).

It is based on a philosophy of transcendence of the individual, the blurring of his or her boundaries, and the continuity between "inside" and "outside" that the concept of the common heritage becomes "natural," and therefore acceptable, because ownership and sovereignty become as open and permeable as the individual.

This connection is old. It was familiar to Gautama Buddha 2,500 years ago. "It is because people cherish the idea of an ego-personality that they cling to the idea of possession," he taught, "but since there is no such thing as an 'ego,' there can be no such things as possessions. When

126

people are able to realize this truth, they will be able to realize the truth of 'non-duality'."

Utilization of resources for the common good and for the private good become identical because there can be no private good without the common good, since the individual is part of the whole.

As Peter Serracino Inglott put it in a recent UNESCO study: "Conflict between individual urges and species are therefore *internal* to the individual. Seeking the good of the species arises from the *depth* of man."[20] A number of consequences flow from this basic concept.

First, we are part of a whole, and we are part of nature. The way we look upon or treat nature is the way we look upon or treat ourselves. The conservation of nature is self-conservation, and the domination and degradation of nature is self-enslavement and debasement.

Scholar and natural philosopher Sidney Holt points out in a study for the same UNESCO project that manifestations of this concept are becoming more numerous. Thus "The Preamble of the World Charter for Nature recognizes that 'Mankind is a part of nature. . . .' Indeed public policies to protect biological diversity, like policies to protect human value, reflect cultural and religious concepts that *extend the definition of self to include nonhuman life* [italics added]."[21] Here again, one of the teachings of Buddha comes to mind: "To best serve one's parents one must learn to practice kindness toward all animate life."

Second, if mankind is part of nature, if the definition of self includes nonhuman life, and if to best serve one's parents one must learn to practice kindness toward all animate life, it then follows that there is an unbreakable continuity between ecology and economy. In Chapter 3, this continuity was stressed from a pragmatic point of view. The philosophy of the common heritage confirms it at the conceptual level.

Third, our traditional *hierarchical* concept of nature is reflected in a hierarchical concept of human society and

vice versa. With anthropocentric certitude, mankind envisaged a scale of evolution from lower to higher forms of
life and from lower intelligence to higher intelligence, the
highest intelligence being that closest to human intelligence and therefore understandable to us. The current
neo-Socratic awareness among scientists that the more we
know the more we become aware of how little we know
should contribute to changing this perception of hierarchy.

The measurement and quantification of intelligence pose
insoluble problems even when applied to humans. IQ tests
were originally devised to identify suitable candidates for
the French bureaucracy. "Intelligence" as quantified by
these tests is more a manifestation of successful adaptation
to determined standards and subcultures than of creative
intelligence.

If we cannot measure human intelligence, how can we
arrogate to ourselves the capacity to quantify and classify
animal intelligence? Our ignorance about what goes on in
an animal mind is abysmal. When we fail to understand
the incredible "intelligence" of migrating fish or turtles or
birds in finding their way across the planet through night
and fog, we think we solve the problem by calling it
"instinct."

We are only beginning to have an inkling about commu-
nications among animals. We recognize their "technology"
(radar in bats, sonar in sharks, aerodynamics in birds, air-
conditioning in termites, etc.) only after we have "invented"
or, rather, "rediscovered" it ourselves. We know little about
their "sixth sense," their prescience in time and across space,
of danger or death, of departures and arrivals.

"Instinct," according to traditional wisdom, is built into
the species—is, it is innate and is not learned individually.
But once the perceived barrier between the species and the
individual has crumbled, so has the distinction between
instinct and intelligence. Learning and innateness are as
difficult to separate as heredity and environment in individual behavior.

Evolution is not a one-dimensional process; it is four-dimensional in a space-time continuum—synchronous, as all stages of evolution are still around us in the biosphere; diachronic, changing through time; and microchronous within each one of us as "human embryos are at some stage like fish embryos and very much like reptilean embryos."[22] And the intelligence in nature around us may be as high as our own, even if it is so different from our own that we simply fail to grasp it.

Such a concept of nature is, obviously, not hierarchical, and is reflected in a concept of humanity that is not hierarchical but open and four-dimensional in a dynamic space-time continuum, the time dimension including the short term as well as the long term. The short term corresponds to narrow space—the "individual" or limited group—and may be laden with conflict. What a distortion by the Social Darwinists, however, to take the infinitesimal for the integral, and to announce that conflict is the law of nature and the basis of progressive evolution! If conflict were the rule of nature, life could not have moved beyond the protozoan stage. Conflict may prevail in the very short term, but the basic force of evolution is cooperation and integration no matter whether we look at cultural or at biological evolution. Lonely cavemen we would be. There would be no cities, no cultures, no accumulation, and no common heritage if conflict were the law of nature. Conflict is sporadic and limited in space and time. Cooperation is the basic long-term principle.

This view of nature, then, is reflected in the concept of a nonhierarchical (i.e., democratic) and, in the long term, nonconflictual (i.e., cooperative) society. A cooperative social order can only be based on this kind of natural philosophy.

Fourth, the openness and permeability of the individual—the osmosis between "inside" and "outside"—has its counterpart at the collective and institutional levels. There is an unbreakable continuity between internal and external

129

issues and policies. Internal policymaking is continually constrained by developments beyond the control of the national lawmaker. Foreign policy is constrained by internal sectoral interests. An open and democratic internal political order is reflected in an open and democratic internal policy. Tyranny and oppression internally generate aggression and oppression at the international level. A revolutionary, rhetorical quest for a new, equitable international economic order, based on feudalism and oppression and disregard for life at home, constitutes a pathology that cannot be productive. A new, equitable economic order must be intranational as well as international, or it will not be at all.

Fifth, a sectoral approach to policymaking is articulated in separate government departments which often lack the instruments for proper coordination and integration of policies. As a result, frequently the left hand does not know what the right hand is doing. This has its counterpart in the sectoral structure of international institutions and in proliferating international bureaucracies which duplicate efforts and are incapable of generating an integrated concept of policymaking. The realignment taking place in many countries within governments, resulting in "departments of ocean development" intended as fora for making integrated ocean policy, will be reflected in an institutional realignment toward integration at the international level.

Sixth, the ecology-economy continuum, as well as the permeability of the "individual" unit and the blurring of its contours, are reflected in a continuity of institutions from the local and national to the regional and international levels. Interaction between these levels must be properly articulated: the field of ocean management provides an example. Conflict and cooperation at this institutional level are functions of time. Perceived conflict between local interests, or local and national interests, or national and regional interests, are short range and random in nature. In the long term, there cannot be any conflict between the part and the whole, and the well-being of the whole depends on the well-being of its weakest part.

Seventh, the time scale of policy options is a function of their scale in space. Local options may be short term and random. National options are medium term, and regional options must be seen as longer term. Global options necessarily include future generations, which equally form part of mankind, conceived, according to Sidney Holt, as a "four-dimensional species" in a space-time continuum.

Eighth, long-term planning, including planning for the well-being of future generations, is difficult to achieve through institutions that reflect narrow sectoral interests and groups prone to frequent changes. Long-term planning can be achieved only on a broad, permanent basis of popular participation outlasting ephemeral changes in government. (There is, of course, as yet little empirical support for the thesis that broad-based popular participation in long-term planning would be successful. Without such participation, however, it cannot take place at all.) The longer the scope, the broader is the need for participation. Long-term planning, which reconciles perceived short-term conflicts between parts and whole, must have grass roots and must be articulated in democratic processes, interlinking local, national, regional, and global institutions and reflecting a nonanthropocentric view of nature that is nonhierarchical, four-dimensional, continuous, and permeable.

These considerations are somewhat sketchy and impressionistic. They should be elaborated and integrated into a coherent *Weltanschauung,* a view of ourselves in our environment that is both new and old and that departs from uniquely Europocentric, Western tradition and attempts to blend Western scientific values with Eastern philosophical values.

In a philosophy of this sort, the concept of the common heritage of mankind is truly at home. For it is a philosophy of nonownership: the common heritage cannot be appropriated.

It is a philosophy of nonconflict: the common heritage is reserved for exclusively peaceful purposes.

It is a philosophy of participation and equity: the common heritage requires a system of management in which all users participate, and it requires sharing of benefits.

It is a philosophy that respects the rights of future generations. And the common heritage concept postulates the conservation of resources for future generations.

The slowly emerging new international order will draw heavily on the new Law of the Sea. References to the Law of the Sea are ubiquitous in all sectors of the development of international law and cooperation. Yet the Law of the Sea, though incomplete, has gone further than any other existing law in institutionalizing a philosophy of nature. The Law of the Sea is, in a way, a philosophy of nature, for "law" is a part of philosophy and "the sea" is nature. Elaboration of the Law of the Sea is bringing us continuously face to face with living creatures in their environment. It obliges us to define our attitude toward them, and this involves, together with the lawyer and economist, the natural scientist, who traditionally is a philosopher of nature. Given the enormous responsibility attributed by the new Law of the Sea to science and scientists, it is not surprising that there is a growing demand among the scientists for a charter that complements the Convention on the Law of the Sea. Such a charter for the seas and oceans would be a declaration not of law but of ethical principles, open to signature by organizations of scientists and individual citizens everywhere. It would express and give rise to the kind of broad grass-roots support needed for ratification of the Convention on the Law of the Sea and the formulation and implementation of long-term planning for future generations—planning on a time scale commensurate with the immensity of the oceans.

René Dupuy of the Collège de France has proposed such

a charter. The international community, he suggests, "deems it necessary that decisions should be made, under UNESCO auspices, and with the assistance of the competent agencies of the United Nations family, on courses of action *to change man's perception of the seas and oceans* and help him to take cognizance of his duty to adjust his mental and intellectual attitudes and his behaviour to the requirements of the maritime situation."[23]

He points out that the "cultural and ethical aspects of man's interaction with the seas and oceans have not yet been given thorough attention," and that there is a need for research and education.[23] Man has the right to knowledge regarding the seas and oceans, and it is the duty of educational institutions to give a notion of the beauty of the maritime universe and its role in poetry, music, and the figurative arts, as well as in the life and livelihood of people.

The physical oneness of the world ocean, which transcends legal divisions, constitutes a link that should enhance a feeling of solidarity among all people. Just as physically the ocean is a moderating influence in coastal regions, tempering, as it were, the harshness of temperature contrasts prevalent in internal continental climes, it should also have an equalizing, tempering influence on nations' economic fortunes, offering to countries poor in land-based resources an alternative resource base and a share in the management of the common heritage. Mankind has a right to a healthy marine environment, Dupuy stresses, and a right to rational management of marine economic resources.

If the seas and oceans must be used exclusively for peaceful purposes, it is the duty of educational institutions everywhere to instill the idea, from early childhood on, that the seas and oceans are *zones of peace*.

The right to the development of marine scientific research for exclusively peaceful purposes, the right of the maritime worker—whether sailor, fisherman, or miner—

to make a decent living and to safety at sea, and the right to information on ocean affairs conclude the list of Dupuy's proposed rights and duties which should be included in a charter for the seas and oceans. "The place occupied by the seas and oceans in the economic and social development of peoples must be given enhanced significance in the context of the new international information order," he states.[23]

The elaboration and adoption of such a declaration of ethical principles would in itself have a considerable educational impact and confront leading scientists with the basic issues of the philosophy of the common heritage. The propagation of the declaration or charter and the gathering of signatures would constitute a second educational effort, while its implementation through scientific, civic, and educational institutions, national and international, would sustain this educational effort and contribute to the effective implementation and further development of the Convention on the Law of the Sea as a model for, and part of, a new international order.

A sustained educational effort is needed to ensure that our whole attitude toward the ocean will change, informed by a new concept of the interrelation between the individual and the intranational and international order and between the socioeconomic order and nature.

An order inspired by such a philosophy might be viable. It might absorb the new phase of the industrial revolution and solve some of the most urgent problems of development, disarmament, and the conservation of the environment. New problems will undoubtedly arise. These, too, are part of the common heritage, to be bequeathed, together with their rights, to future generations.

Notes

1. Malahoff, A. 1982. Sea Technology. Vol. 23, No. 1.
2. Lonkarevic, B.D. 1972. Prospects for Deepsea Mining. Address to the First Canadian Science Writers Workshop. January 1–15.
3. UNESCO. 1983. Ocean Science for the Year 2000. Report of an Expert Consultation Organized by SCOR/ACMRR with the Support of IOC and the Division of Marine Sciences of UNESCO (IOC/INFO. 505). Paris: UNESCO.
4. Isaccs, J.D., and W. R. Schmitt. 1980. Ocean energy: Forms and prospects. Science 207(4428):265–273.
5. Pardo, A. 1983. Law of the Sea. Development, Journal of the Society for International Development. 2:7.
6. Giarini, O. 1982. Dialogue on Wealth and Welfare. Oxford: Pergamon.
7. Anonymous. 1983. Barter on the Upswing in Consequence of Debt Crisis. Süddeutsche Zeitung. December 20.
8. Pardo, A. 1975. The Common Heritage. Selected Papers on Oceans and World Order, 1967–1974. Malta: University of Malta Press, 1975.
9. Boisson, P. 1981. La sécurité en mer. Dunkerque, France: Graphic Foto Edition.
10. Borgese, E.M., ed. Pacem in Maribus, Vol. XII. (Forthcoming)
11. Calder, R. 1974. Center Magazine. Nov./Dec., p. 35.
12. Borgese, E.M., ed. 1971. An ocean development tax. Pacem in Maribus, Vol. III. Planning and Development in the Oceans. Malta: The Royal University of Malta Press.
13. Castanēda, J. 1971. In: Pacem in Maribus, Vol. II, E.M. Borgese, ed. Malta: International Ocean Institute.
14. Beesley, J.A. 1971. In: Pacem in Maribus, Vol. II, E.M. Borgese, ed. Malta: International Ocean Institute.
15. Brucan, S. 1971. In: Pacem in Maribus, Vol. II, E.M. Borgese, ed. Malta: International Ocean Institute.

16. Oda, S. 1983. Fisheries under the United Nations Convention on the Law of the Sea. American Journal of International Law. Vol. 77, No. 4.
17. Kent, G. 1980. The Politics of Pacific Island Fisheries. Boulder, Colo.: Westview Press.
18. Glendinen, D. 1984. Tenfold Rise in Oil Lost at Sea Reported for 1983. New York Times. October 7.
19. Economic Commission for Latin America. 1981. Regional Programme of Action for Latin America. Montevideo: ECLA.
20. Inglott, P.S. 1981. The Rights of Future Generations: Some Socio-Philosophical Considerations. UNESCO Working Paper. Paris: UNESCO.
21. Holt, S. 1982. Towards Ensuring the Rights of Future Generations: Scientific Aspects. UNESCO Working Paper. Paris: UNESCO. [United Nations. 1982. World Charter for Nature. 48th Plenary Meeting, General Assembly, United Nations, New York, October 28.]
22. Medawar, P. 1983. The evidence of evolution. Pp. 49–50 in: Darwin's Legacy, C.L. Hamrum, ed. New York: Harper & Row.
23. Dupuy, R. UNESCO Working Paper Paris: UNESCO.

Select
Bibliography

Alexander, L.M. 1981. Organizational responses to new ocean science and technology developments. Ocean Development and International Law 9(3/4):241–268.

Bardach, J.E., J.H. Ryther, and W.O. McLarney. 1972. Aquaculture: The Farming and Husbandry of Fresh-water and Marine Organisms. New York: Wiley-Interscience.

Borgese, E.M. 1968. The Ocean Regime. Santa Barbara, Calif.: Center for the Study of Democratic Institutions.

———. 1976. The Drama of the Oceans. New York: Harry Abrams.

———. 1981. Seafarm: The Story of Aquaculture. New York: Harry Abrams.

———. 1985. The Mines of Neptune. New York: Harry Abrams.

———, and N. Ginsburg, eds. 1979–1985. Ocean Yearbook, Vols. I–V. Chicago: University of Chicago Press.

Charney, J.I. 1975. Revenue sharing. Policy Issues in Ocean Law. Washington, D.C.: The American Society of International Law.

Cronan, D.S. 1980. Underwater Minerals. New York: Academic Press.

Dalhousie Oceans Studies Programme. 1982. Third United Nations Conference on the Law of the Sea. Dalhousie Ocean Studies Programme, Dalhousie University, Halifax, Nova Scotia.

Kent, P. 1980. Minerals from the Marine Environment. London: Edward Arnold.

Pardo, A., and E.M. Borgese. 1976. The New International Economic Order and the Law of the Sea. International Ocean Institute Occasional Papers, No. 4, Malta.

Platzöder, R. 1974–1982. Third United Nations Conference on the Law of the Sea. Documents. Ebenhausen: Stiftung Wissenschaft und Politik.

Post, A. 1983. Deepsea Mining and the Law of the Sea. The Hague: Martinus Nijhoff.

Ross, D. 1980. Opportunities and Uses of the Ocean. New York: Springer-Verlag.

Saqat, S.S. 1978. The Kuwait Convention for Co-operation on the Protection from Pollution of the Marine Environment and the Arabian Gulf Area. Revue égyptienne de droit international. 34:149–159.

Shusterich, K. 1982. Resource Management and the Oceans. The Political Economy of Sea-bed Mining. Boulder, Colo.: Westview Press.

Index - Future of Oceans

AAAS. *See* American Association for the Advancement of Science

Africa, 26, 83, 89

American Association for the Advancement of Science (AAAS), 33. *See also* Science

Antarctica, xiv, 26, 68; continental shelf of, 82-3; module regime, 122

Aquaculture: 14-25; economics of, 58-9

Arab states, 83

Arctic, 26

Argentina, 80

Aristotle, 25

Asia, 89. *See also* Southeast Asia

Asian-African Legal Consultative Committee, 117-19

Atlantic Ocean, 7, 26, 29, 39

Australia, 11-12, 80

Austria, 55

Baltic Sea, 61

Bay of Fundy, 39

Beesley, J. Alan, 64

Boisson, Philippe, 59

Borgese, Elisabeth Mann, ix, xii

Brazil, 110

Britain, 39-40. *See also* England

British Columbia, 8, 84

British Oil Spill Intelligence Report, 103, 105

Brucan, Silviu, 64

Buddha, 3, 126-7

Calder, Lord Ritchie, 62

California, 21, 25, 80

Camus, Albert, 74

Canada: Bay of Fundy tidal plant, 39; continental shelf of, 80; and ocean development tax, 64-5, 84

Castañeda, Jorge, 64

Charter of Economic Rights and Duties of States, 117

China: aquaculture in, 14, 19, 23; community farming in, 58; and tidal power, 39

Club of Rome, ix, xi, xiv, 44

Committee on the Peaceful Uses of the Sea-bed, the Ocean Floor and the Subsoil thereof Beyond the Limits of National Jurisdiction, 1968-1973, 64

Common Heritage: economics of, 2-3, 43-68, 71, 77; and the high seas, 85-6, 93-4, 98, 100; philosophy of, 125-134; principal of, 1; and scientific research, 107; in U.N. convention, 70

Common Heritage Fund, 65

Congo, 41

Convention on the Prohibition of Military or Any Other Hostile Use of Environmental Modification Techniques, 105

Convention on the Territorial Sea and the Contiguous Zone, 75

Cormorant Field (U.K.), 26

Creole Field (Gulf of Mexico), 25

Cyprus, 8

Deducted Value, 45-9
Dialogue on Wealth and Welfare, 44. *See also* Giarini, Orio
Dowry and Patrimony, 45-55, 58, 66
D&P. *See* Dowry and Patrimony
Dupuy, René, 132-4

Echeverria, Luis, 125
ECLA. *See* Economic Commission for Latin America
Economic Commission for Latin America (ECLA), 116-17
Ecuador, 11, 76
EEC. *See* European Economic Community
EEZ. *See* Exclusive Economic Zone
Einstein, Albert, 44, 68
El Niño, 11-12
Energy, 38-42. *See also* Ocean Thermal Energy Conversion (OTEC)
England, 25
Enterprise, 94-7. *See also* International Sea-bed Authority (ISA)
Esso, 26
European Economic Community (EEC), 98-9
European Human Rights Court, 109
Exclusive Economic Zone (EEZ), 62, 65-6, 76-9, 84-90

FAO. *See* Food and Agriculture Organization of the United Nations
Fiji, 76
Food and Agriculture Organization of the United Nations (FAO), 18, 62, 63, 88, 109, 117, 119, 122
France, 31
Franciscan Philosophy, 125

Galapagos: islands, x, 84; ridge, 7-8
Genesis, 6
Geneva Convention. *See* United Nations Conference on the Law of the Sea
Germany (Federal republic), 98
Giarini, Orio: 44-52; theory as applied to the oceans, 52-4, 58-60, 62
Glaude, George, 41
Golob, Richard, 105
Gulf Stream, 40

Hague, The, conventions of 1907, 104
Hanseatic League of Port States, 101
Hawaii, 41
Heden, Carl Gören, 21
Holt, Sidney, 127

ILO. *See* International Labour Organization
IMO. *See* International Maritime Organization
India, 25, 58, 80
Indian Ocean: 61, 102, 117; and polymetallic nodules, 29
Indonesia, 11, 58, 76
Inglott, Peter Serracino, 127
Inmarsat, 99
Intelsat, 99
Intergovernmental Oceanographic Commission (IOC), 62, 63, 88, 114, 117, 119
International Court of Justice, 67, 109
International Labour Organization (ILO), 88
International Maritime Organization (IMO), 63, 88, 109, 119
International Ocean Institute (Malta), xiv

International Sea-bed Authority (ISA): 1-2, 36; Assembly of State Members, 95; council of, 95-96; Economic Planning Commission, 95; Legal and Technical Commission, 95; organization of, 95-100; Preparatory Commission, 55-6, 69, 71, 82-4, 89, 93-6; review conference, 97; Secretariat, 97, 123

International Tribunal for the Law of the Sea, 2, 55, 89, 109, 110, 116

IOC. *See* Intergovernmental Oceanographic Commission

ISA. *See* International Sea-bed Authority

Iran, 102-3

Iraq, 102

Isaacs, J.D., 41-2

Japan: 19, 31, 41; and sea coal, 29, 59

JEFERAD. *See* Joint Venture for Exploration, Research and Development

Joint Venture for Exploration, Research and Development (JEFERAD), 55

Juan de Fuca Ridge, 7

Kent, George, 78

Keynesianism, 44, 50

Kissinger, Henry, 97

Lao-tse, 74

La securité en mer, 59

Latin America, 89. *See also* Regional Programme of Action for Latin America

Law of the Sea: xii-xiv; and common heritage, 3; as philosophy of nature, 132

Law of the Sea Secretariat of the United Nations, 119

Lonkarevic, B.D., 8

Louisiana, 80

Libya, 34

Malahoff, Alexander, 8

Malaysia, 68

Malta, 1, 72, 83

Massachusetts Institute of Technology, 33

Mediterranean Sea, 7, 61

Mexico, 34, 64

Miami, 40

More, Sir Thomas, 73

Mozambique, 29

NASA. *See* United States National Aeronautics and Space Administration

Nepal, 65

Newfoundland, 84

NOAA. *See* United States National Oceanic and Atmospheric Administration

North America, 12

North Sea, 26

North-South, 93-95, 99

Ocean Development Tax, 63-6, 79, 83-4, 99, 107-8

Ocean Mining: economics of, 54-8; and polymetallic nodules, 7-9, 25-38; systems of, 31-2

Ocean Science for the Year 2000 (UNESCO), 10

Ocean Thermal Energy Conversion (OTEC), 40-1, 67

Oda, Shigeru, 67

Oregon, 8, 84

OTEC. *See* Ocean Thermal Energy Conversion

Pacific Islands, 41, 84

141

Pacific Ocean: 7, 8, 11, 61; and polymetallic nodules, 29, 32
Pardo, Arvid, xiii, 43, 52-3, 72
Peccei, Aurelio, ix, 38, 44
Persian Gulf, 26, 102-6
Peru, 76
Philippines, 19, 76
Plato, 73
Pollution: biological control of, 21, 38; as deducted value, 45; economics of, 66, 72; and energy resources, 38-9; greenhouse effect, xii; and heavy metals, 9, 14; marine environment, 101-6; monitoring and surveillance of, 59-61; in the Persian Gulf, 101-3; and recycling and waste utilization (utilization value), 46-8

Qatar, 102

Rance River, 39
Reagan Administration, 98
Reciprocating States Agreement, 98-9
Red Sea, 7, 32
Regional Commission for Ocean Development and Environment, 114-6
Regional Organization for the Protection of the Marine Environment, 102
Regional Programme of Action for Latin America, 116-7
Regional Seas Programme, 61, 62, 64, 88-91, 101-3, 104, 108, 119. *See also* United Nations Environment Programme
Romania, 49, 64

Sahel, 12
Saint-Malo tidal power plant, 39
Saudi Arabia, 102
Schmitt, W.R., 41-2

Science, 33, 41
Shell, 26
South America, 26
Southeast Asia, 12, 33
Soviet Union, 6, 62, 82
Stockholm Conference on the Human Environment of 1972, 88
Süddeutsche Zeitung, 49
Surtsey, 86

Texas, 80
Thyssen, 49
Toffler, Alvin, 34
Tolstoy, Leo, 62
Treaty on the Prohibition of the Emplacement of Nuclear Weapons and Other Weapons of Mass Destruction on the Sea-bed and the Ocean Floor and in the Subsoil Thereof, 73, 100, 110
Truman Declaration, 80-1

Ui, Jun, 59
UNCLOS. *See* United Nations Conference on the Law of the Sea
UNCTAD. *See* United Nations Conference on Trade and Development
Underwater Manifold Center Production System, 26
UNDP. *See* United Nations Development Programme
UNEP. *See* United Nations Environment Programme
UNESCO. *See* United Nations Educational, Scientific and Cultural Organization
UNIDO. *See* United Nations Industrial Development Organization
United Kingdom, 98. *See also* England and Britain

142

United Nations, 52
United Nations Conference on Trade and Development (UNCTAD), 57, 88
United Nations Conference on the Law of the Sea (UNCLOS): xii-xiv, 1, 55, 62, 64-5, 67, 71-5, 81-2, 87-90, 93, 111, 123, 125; Preparatory Commission, 1-2, 36-7, 55-6, 57; Resolution I, 1-2; Resolution II, 1
United Nations Convention on the Law of the Sea (1982), 1, 4, 36, 43-4, 53-5, 61, 65-6, 69-91, 93, 95, 97-9, 101, 103, 107-112, 116, 132, 134
United Nations Development Programme (UNDP), 57, 88, 105
United Nations Educational, Scientific and Cultural Organization (UNESCO), 88, 109, 114, 117, 127
United Nations Environment Programme (UNEP), 61, 69, 88-9, 103, 109. See also Regional Seas Programme
United Nations General Assembly, 43, 123
United Nations Industrial Development Organization (UNIDO), 57, 108

United Nations Revolving Fund for the Exploration of Hard Minerals and Geothermal Energy in Developing Countries, 37, 57
United Nations Secretariat, 117
United Nations Security Council, 109
United States, 6, 96, 98, 99
United States National Aeronautics and Space Administration (NASA), 21
United States National Oceanic and Atmospheric Administration (NOAA), 7
University of Hawaii, 78
University of Miami, 21
University of Tokyo, 59
Utilization Value, 46-8, 49, 66-7

Valdivia, 29
Venezuela, 73

Washington (state), 8, 84
Wegener, Alfred, 6
Weltanschauung, 131
Wilcox, Howard A., 21, 40
World Charter for Nature, 127
World Bank, 57

Zaire, 57
Zambia, 57
Zimbabwe, 57

The Author

Elisabeth Mann Borgese, the daughter of Thomas and Katja Mann, was born in Munich in 1918 and emigrated with her eminent parents to Switzerland and the United States during the Nazi period. In the U.S.A. she was long associated with The Center for the Study of Democratic Institutions at Santa Barbara and published widely on questions related to the law of the sea, ocean management and ecology. Since 1980, she has been a professor of Political Science at Dalhousie University in Halifax, Chairman, Planning Council, International Ocean Institute, and Vice-director of The Pearson Institute, all at Dalhousie. Her previous books include: *To Whom It May Concern* (1962), *Ascent of Women* (1963), *The Language Barrier* (1965), *The Ocean Regime* (1968), *The Drama of the Oceans* (1976), *Seafarm: The Story of Aquaculture* (1980), and *The Mines of Neptune* (1985).